I0661604

Ralph Nicholson Wornum

Analysis of Ornament, Characteristics of Styles

An Introduction to the Study of the History of Ornamental Art

Ralph Nicholson Wornum

Analysis of Ornament, Characteristics of Styles
An Introduction to the Study of the History of Ornamental Art

ISBN/EAN: 9783337140083

Printed in Europe, USA, Canada, Australia, Japan

Cover: Foto ©Andreas Hilbeck / pixelio.de

More available books at **www.hansebooks.com**

ANALYSIS OF ORNAMENT

THE

CHARACTERISTICS OF STYLES

AN INTRODUCTION TO THE STUDY OF THE HISTORY OF ORNAMENTAL ART

By RALPH N. WORNUM

KEEPER AND SECRETARY, NATIONAL GALLERY

SIXTH EDITION

LONDON
CHAPMAN AND HALL, 193, PICCADILLY
1879

[*The right of Translation is reserved.*]

LONDON:
PRINTED BY VIRTUE AND CO., LIMITED,
CITY ROAD.

PREFACE TO THE FIRST EDITION.

THE following Sketch is prepared chiefly as an introductory guide to aid in the adoption of some ready system in the study of Ornament. Though illustrated ornamental works exist in great profusion, they are generally on special monuments and localities, or extending only over very limited periods of time: and being, further, mostly of a purely illustrative character, without analytical description of the parts, they fail to impress on the mind of the Student those elements which are the essential characteristics of the works, and distinguish their style. These characteristics, therefore, which are the very essence of the Art, are to be apprehended only by dint of great labour in the comparison of many costly publications, which, until lately, have been generally inaccessible even to the metropolitan Student. But with access to such works, some systematic general guide is absolutely indispensable to enable the Student to acquire a sound apprehension of his subject, with moderate labour, and within a moderate time.

The knowledge of ornamental style is, doubtless, most readily imparted in a course of lectures, in which, by numerous illustrations on a large scale, including occasionally the objects themselves, the peculiar features of each style can be at once pointed out, and fixed on the mind, through the facilities of immediate comparison. But this compendious abstract of the course of Lectures on

Ornamental Art,—delivered by me originally at Somerset
House ; and subsequently at Marlborough House, under the
direction of the Board of Trade Department of Science and
Art,—in the absence of a more complete report, may serve
in some measure as a substitute for the personal instructions
of a lecture, by pointing out its sources, and enabling the
Student to derive directly from the standard authorities in
the Library of the Department such information for himself. The Student will find the most important works illustrating the subject enumerated in the text, to which he
must refer for its complete illustration ; but he will find
the most essential and characteristic elements of the styles,
perhaps adequately illustrated by the few engraved cuts
contained in the work, which have been chiefly executed
from casts in the collections of the Department, by the
female students of the Wood-engraving Class at Marlborough House.

The accompanying Sketch, however, is not published as
a report of the Lectures referred to : it is simply a concise
abstract of their substance, and is intended only as an
introductory aid for the Student, to enable him to make
profitable use of the works in the Library, in furtherance
of an earnest study of Ornamental Art.*

R. N. W.

July, 1855.

---

* See the *Account of the Library, &c., with a Catalogue of the principal
Works, classified for the use of the Visitors.* By Ralph N. Wornum,
Librarian. London, 1855. The diagrams prepared by me for these
lectures now form part of the property of this Library. The Lectures
were originally delivered in the Government Schools of Design, both at
Somerset House and in the provincial schools in England, Scotland,
and Ireland, in the years 1848, 1849, and 1850.

INTRODUCTION.

ORNAMENT.

CHAPTER I.

THE history of art shows two great classes of ornamental styles—the *symbolic* and the *æsthetic;* that is, those which appeal to our understandings, and those which appeal to our feelings. We may term those styles symbolic in which the ordinary elements have been chosen for the sake of their significations, as symbols of something not necessarily implied, and irrespective of their effect as works of art, or arrangements of forms and colours. Those that are composed of elements devised solely from principles of symmetry of form and harmony of colour, and exclusively for their effect on our *perception of the beautiful*, without any further extraneous or ulterior aim, may be termed æsthetic.

Style in ornament is analogous to *hand* in writing, and this is its literal signification. As every individual has some peculiarity in his mode of writing, so every age or nation has been distinguished in its ornamental expression by a certain individuality of taste, either original or borrowed. It is the comprehension of these individual tastes,

B

characterizing various times and people, which must constitute the most thorough education of the ornamental designer. These expressions are interesting also to the general student, as they exhibit an essential quality of the social character of these different people, both in relation to the arts and to general culture and religion.

In a review of these ornamental styles we shall find that the elements of form are constant in all cases; they are but variously treated. This, in fact, must be so, if a style be founded upon any principles at all; and those styles which have carried with them the feelings of ages could not be otherwise than based upon some fixed natural laws.

The elements of styles are of two kinds—pure and absolute, and conventional and arbitrary; or natural and fanciful.

The investigation of the principles of ornamental art is an inquiry into the nature and character of these elements: how the effects of certain variations of form and colour happen to be so universally appreciated that the varieties of their arrangements have occupied all people from the remotest times.

Universal efforts show a universal want; and beauty of effect and decoration are no more a luxury in a civilised state of society than warmth and clothing are a luxury to any state: the mind, as the body, makes everything necessary that it is capable of permanently enjoying. Ornament is one of the mind's necessities, which it gratifies by means of the eye; and, in its strictest æsthetic sense, it has a perfect analogy with music, which similarly gratifies the mind, but by the means of a different organ—the ear.

So ornament has been discovered to be again an essential

element in commercial prosperity. This was not so at first, because, in a less cultivated state, we are quite satisfied with the gratification of our merely physical wants. But in an advanced state, the more extensive wants of the mind demand still more pressingly to be satisfied. Hence, ornament is now as material an interest in a commercial community as even cotton itself, or, indeed, any raw material of manufacture whatever.

Such being the case, it is highly important that we should endeavour to comprehend its principles, in order to its most effectual application. We should, therefore, in the first place, study ornament, for its own sake, theoretically and scientifically, and not in that limited narrow sense which would restrict it in one place as applied to cotton, in another as to iron, and in a third as to clay, and so on.

There is most certainly but one road to efficiency for the designer—for the weaver, for the printer, or for the modeller. Their common object is a familiar mastery of ornamental art, in order that they may apply it to the utmost advantage to their respective pursuits. In early stages of manufactures, it is mechanical fitness that is the object of competition. As society advances, it is necessary to combine elegance with fitness; and those who cannot see this must be content to send their wares to the ruder markets of the world, and resign the great marts of commerce to men of superior taste and sounder judgment, who *deserve* a higher reward. This is no new idea. Let us take a lesson from the experience of past ages. The vari-coloured glass of Egypt, the figured cups of Sidon, the shawls of Miletus, the terra-cottas of Samos, the bronzes of Corinth, did not command the markets of the ancient world either for their materials or for their mechanical qualities; not because they were well blown, cleverly chased, finely woven, ingeniously turned, or perfectly cast, —these qualities they had only in common with the similar wares of other nations,—but in the gratification of one of the most refined necessities of the mind in an advanced social state, they were pre-eminent—they were objects of an elegant, cultivated taste. It is by this æsthetic character alone, that manufacturers will ever establish that substantial renown which will insure a lasting market in the civilised world.

When, however, manufactures have attained a high mechanical perfection, or have completely met the necessities of the body, the energy that brought them to that perfection *must* either stagnate or be continued in a higher province—that of taste; for there is a stage of cultivation when the mind must revolt at a mere crude utility. So it is a natural propensity to decorate or embellish whatever is useful or agreeable to us. But just as there are mechanical laws which regulate all our efforts in pure uses, so there are laws of the mind which must regulate those æsthetical efforts expressed in the attempt at decoration or ornamental design.

The production and application of ornament are distinct processes, though they cannot be separated in applied design. A proper distinction between a picture or a model and an ornament is quite essential in the mind of the designer; for the mere power of imitation of natural objects, and even their exact imitation, is perfectly compatible with the total ignorance of ornamental art. The great art of the designer is in the selection and arrangement of his materials, not in their execution. There is a distinct *study of ornament* wholly independent of the merely preliminary exercises of drawing, colouring, or modelling. A designer might even produce a perfect arrangement of forms and colours, and yet show the grossest stupidity in its application.

There are two provinces of ornament—the flat and the relieved. In the flat, we have a contrast of light and dark; in the relieved, a contrast of light and shade; in both, a variety of effect for the pure gratification of the sense of vision. Much is common to both; but in the first case, a play of line is the main feature, in the second, a play of masses, and colour may be an auxiliary to either; but it acts with far greater power in the flat, as it is entirely dependent upon light.

Ornament, therefore, is a system of contrasts: the object of study is the order of contrasts. The individual orders may vary to infinity, though the classes are limited, as right-line or curved-line series, series of simple curves or clustered curves, series of mere lines, or natural objects, as flowers arranged in the orders of these different series. For example, the common scroll is a series of spirals to the right and left alternately; the Roman scroll is the Acanthus plant or brank-ursine, treated in this order of curved series.

CHAPTER II.

DECORATION or ornamentation, then, we may assume to be divided into two great classes—the *flat* and the *round*, or what may be otherwise described as *painting* and *modelling*.

That of *painting*, or the flat, is the far more extensive class. It comprises, in the first place, all pictorial decoration,—general costume, drapery, all printed or woven fabrics, mosaic, inlaying, *Boule*-work, enamelling, and, accordingly, many classes of furniture. The relieved, or *modelling*, is limited to building purposes, hardware, certain kinds of furniture, implements, and to jewellery. But everything that is relieved is comprised also in the flat, in one sense, inasmuch as it can be imitated in the flat: this is however not a legitimate use of the flat, as it is really a mere counterfeit of the round.

We may call these two classes, then, the *flat* and the *round*. They have two qualities in common—shape and contrast. The shape in both is given by the outline; the contrast, in the one by light and shade; in the other, by colour, or light and dark. There is no other means of contrast in the flat but that of colour, or light and dark; for when an ornament in the flat is merely an imitation of the round, it belongs strictly to the round: the contrast in the round is effected by light and shade. All tracery—indeed, all figures, in the flat, are mere light and dark: whether the contrast be that of colours or of black and white, whether of a shadow with its ground or of one form with another, the very elemental principle of vision is contrast, and it must, of course, be the basis of all ornamental art.

Round.

Then, if this view be correct, we have but two great principles to study—shape and contrast; or, in all cases, æsthetically, an agreeable variety of those effects which delight the mind by means of the eye. This is more important than would appear at first; for it shows, that whatever other principle we may associate with the ornamental principle, must be kept secondary to *effect*, if we are desirous of making a good design. Introduce what

Flat.

symbols we will, or apply our designs how we will, they must be made subject to the ruling principles of ornament itself, or, however good the symbolism, our design is a mere crudity in art.

This also illustrates the difference between a picture and an ornament. The ornamental principle of symmetry may be introduced into a picture, but it is far from being essential to it; and when this principle is introduced, which it often is, the picture really becomes an ornamental design. This is the character of nearly all pictures in

the earlier epochs of art, and they were generally parts
of ornamental schemes.

Any picture, whatever the subject, which is composed
merely on principles of symmetry and contrast, becomes an
ornament, and any ornamental design in which these two
principles have been made subservient to imitation or
natural arrangement has departed from the province of
ornament into that of the picture or the model, whichever
it may be. And in nearly all designs of this kind, applied
to useful purposes, you frustrate the very principle of
nature, upon which you found your theory, when you
represent a natural form in a natural manner, and yet
apply it to uses with which it has, in nature, no affinity
whatever. Therefore, however you may conform with
Nature in little matters, you certainly commit an outrage
upon her in great matters.

There is a class of ornament which has much increased
of late years in England, and, by way of distinction, we
may call it the *naturalist* school. The theory appears to
be, that as nature is beautiful, ornamental details derived
immediately from beautiful natural objects must insure a
beautiful design. This, however, can only be true where
the original uses of the details chosen have not been
obviously violated; and one peculiar feature of this
school is, that it often substitutes the *ornament itself* for
the thing to be ornamented, as illustrated in the accompanying examples; in which the natural objects are so
mismanaged as to be *principals:* flame proceeding from a
flower, a basket on an animal's head to hold a liquid,
a bell made of leaves! the elements chosen being so
opposed to the proposed uses of the objects ornamented,

as to make the designs simply æsthetic monstrosities, ornamental abominations.

Ornament is essentially the accessory to, and not the

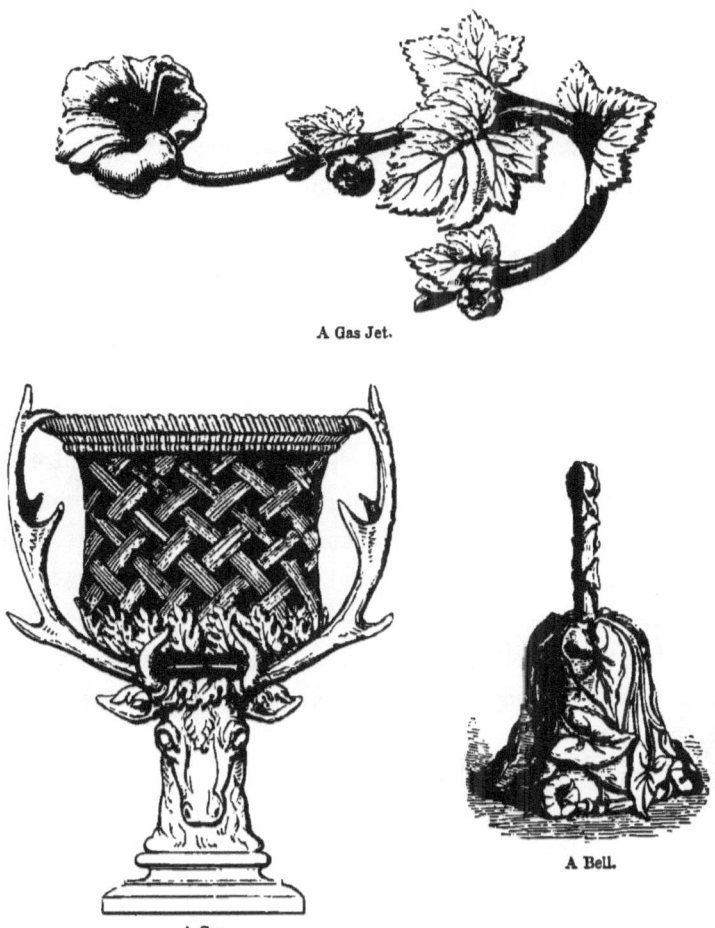

A Gas Jet.

A Cup.

A Bell.

substitute of, the useful; it is a decoration or adornment; it can have no independent existence practically. We cannot look upon any mere ornament without instantly

C

associating it with something that it is fit, or is destined, to adorn ; as a necklace or a bracelet. Even a statuette is not an ornament, unless you associate it with some shelf or other object or support that it may be fit to adorn. If we look upon it as a mere statue or portrait, it is purely a work of fine art, not an ornament; because it is then principal, instead of being accessory, an absolute condition of all ornament. Hence, every implement or article of practical utility, as, for instance, a candlestick, that is composed or built up of natural imitations exclusively or as principals, however poetical the idea may be supposed to be, is practically bad as a design.

There is a very great difference between *ornamenting* a utensil with natural objects, and *substituting* these natural objects for the utensil itself. In the latter case, however true the details, the design is utterly false ; in the former, you are in both respects true, and may be also highly suggestive and instructive. Of course, there are many natural objects which at once suggest certain uses ; and we can never be wrong if we elaborate these into such implements or vessels as their own very forms or natures may have spontaneously presented to the mind.

Every article of use has a certain size and character defined for it by the very use it is destined for, and this may never be disregarded by the designer ; it is, in fact, the indispensable skeleton of his design, and has nothing to do with ornament. But it is upon this skeleton that the designer must bring all his ornamental knowledge to bear ; and he is a poor designer if he can do nothing more than imitate a few sticks and leaves, or other natural objects wherewith to decorate it; he must give it character as well as beauty, and make it suggestive of something more than a display of sprigs and flowers gathered from the fields, or this would be mannerism indeed.

Natural floral ornament is one kind of ornament, and a very beautiful kind; but even an infinite variety of floral detail, especially in the round, will have æsthetically but very little variety of effect upon the mind. For this purpose we must bring *Art* to the aid of *Nature*, or work upon the principles illustrated by natural objects, rather than imitate their individual appearances.

We should add an illustrative elaboration of the abstract principles of beauty, to the mere representation of those natural objects in which they may be most effectively displayed : and this is the professed object of all tracery or mere geometrical design. The beautiful Italian style, known as the Trecento, is a fine example of this combination of natural and artificial forms, in its mixture of conventional flowers and foliage with its tracery and various geometrical designs.

It seems to be a law of nature, that every individual thing shall be composed of two similar parts in its outward appearance; and as the internal arrangement is often different, as in the animal creation, this similarity of externals would appear an evidence of the *design of beauty.* We find this similarity of parts more or less decided according to the individuality of the object—from the simplest crystal form to that of man.

And we find this remarkable similarity relaxed only where its relaxation does not interfere with the beauty of the object,—as in a tree, for instance: the two halves of a tree are not exactly symmetrical in their branches, yet they are generally so. There is quite as much symmetry in every tree as the eye can appreciate.

It is so also with flowers: the calyx and petals of all flowers are symmetrical; and this symmetry is the more decided, inversely as the number of flowers on one stem: plurality of members seems to do away with the special symmetry of the individual member; and where there are several flowers from one root or on one stem, the deviation from individual symmetry is always in favour of the symmetry of the collective group or groups. Where nature groups, it is the *group* that is the ornament, not the individual; and this is a law which must be observed likewise in art; as in all clusters, colonnades, or festoons, the individuals of such designs may be arranged at random, provided the cluster, colonnade, or festoon, be itself of symmetrical proportions.

In endeavouring, therefore, to be symmetrical in our designs, so far from being artificial or formal, we are strictly following one of the grand principles of Nature.

This distinction between the symmetry of the parts and the symmetry of the group or cluster is very important. Take man himself: he is a compound form,—a group of trunk, limbs, and extremities. Whatever part of the group is balanced by a similar member on the other side, is without that symmetry which we are speaking of. The arm is not symmetrical, because it is balanced by a similar member on the other side; but take the head, which has not this plurality to disturb its symmetry, and we find a perfect contrast of the two parts. I believe this to be true of all natural groups; and I believe this law of symmetry to be so important, that there is no form or combination of forms whatever that, when symmetrically contrasted or repeated, cannot be made subservient to beauty.

CHAPTER III.

THE whole grammar of ornament consists in contrast, repetition, and series. A perfect contrast of form may be defined as the two sides of a solid or section of the solid, generated by the revolution of an outline around a given axis; as, for instance, a sphere is the solid generated by the revolution of a semicircle around its diameter.

Repetition and series are nearly identical. Series comprises repetition, and defines its order. Mouldings are simple repetitions, right-lined or curved, as the case may be. Perhaps the best illustration of the value of series is the kaleidoscope. All the beautiful figures represented by that instrument are repetitions in circular series; and often the rudest materials will generate extremely beautiful effects.

And the elliptical, or any other regular series, symmetrically arranged, will be found nearly equally valuable with the circular.

In no popular style of ornament have natural details ever yet prevailed. The details of all great styles are largely derived from nature, but for the most part conventionally treated; and theory and experience seem to show that this is the true system.

A plant is said to be *conventionally* treated, when the natural order of its growth or development is disregarded. Where the exact imitation of the details, and its own order of development, are both observed, the treatment is *natural;* and an object so treated, independent of any application, is only a picture or model, not an ornament: to be an ornament, it must be applied as an accessory decoration to something else.

In Egyptian, Greek, and Roman ornament, it is extremely rare to find any natural treatment of the details: that is, any mere imitation. The only examples I can recall are the birds, reptiles, and animals occasionally introduced in arabesques and scroll-work. The case is the same with Byzantine and Saracenic art, and with the great styles of Italy, especially the Trecento and the Cinquecento, in which all the most perfect schemes are purely conventional, or upon a strict geometrical basis, whatever the treatment of the detail may be.

Lorenzo Ghiberti has introduced exact natural imitations in his celebrated gates of the Baptistery of San Giovanni at Florence; but they are strictly accessory to a general plan, and symmetrically arranged; being neither negligently nor naturally disposed. They are bound in bunches or groups of various shapes and sizes, disposed in harmony with the main compartments of the gates, of which they are ornaments. And this is, perhaps, the utmost extent to which decorations of this class can be judiciously applied. But in Ghiberti's case, as elsewhere, the group is the ornament, and not the parts of which it is composed.

It is requisite that we should have a clear understand-

ing of the difference between a natural and a conventional
or ornamental treatment of an object. A natural treatment implies natural imitation and arrangement; but an
ornamental treatment does not necessarily exclude imitation in the parts; as, for instance, a scroll may be
composed of strictly natural parts; but as no plant would
grow in an exact spiral direction, the scroll form constitutes the ornamental or conventional arrangement. As
in the following arrangement of a leaf, from an old French
example.

We may have, however, conventionalities of details as
well as conventionalities of arrangement. A leaf or a
flower, for instance, may be represented as it appears,
with all the local accidents of light and shade and colour:
this would be a strictly natural representation. And it
may be represented as a mere diagram,—that is, as we
know it to be,—without reference to its appearance; or
it may be treated as a mere shadow of itself,—as a
silhouette: the two latter would be conventional treat-
ments; and it is such representations that we find almost
exclusively in Egyptian and Greek art; as the Lotus
of the Egyptian tombs and temples, or the various foliage
of the terra-cotta vases of Greece.

There can be no question that the motive of ornament is not the presentation of natural images to the mind, but the rendering the object ornamented as agreeable as possible to it, and therefore the details of decoration should have no independent character of their own, but be kept purely subservient to beauty of effect. This can hardly be done, or rather cannot be thoroughly done, but by the adoption of conventional ornament—whether flowers, foliage, or other natural forms: because as a conventional or mere geometrical form can really have no individual associations, and yet at the same time may present an extremely beautiful effect, the whole of that effect is simply auxiliary to the general beauty of the object decorated: the ornamentation is purely accessory. The designer must ever remember that the effect of the whole should never be interfered with by any partial attraction of the details.

Every design is composed of plan and details—as in a vase, the shape of the vase is the plan; whatever decorations it may have are the details of the design, or their enrichments, as medallion pictures or pieces of sculpture: so with a candlestick, casket, and others.

In all cases where elaborate works of Fine Art are

introduced as enrichments of an ornamental scheme—as sculpture in the pediment of a Greek temple, or a picture in the panel of a wall—it is only in the general form and arrangement that they share in the ornamental effect; they are no longer ornaments when examined in detail, but independent works of Fine Art.

The ordinary details or accessory decorations may be of various kinds: they may cover the entire surface of the plan, or only portions of it; the covering of only portions of a plan involves, of course, far higher ornamental principles than the uniform covering the entire surface. Decorations which are spread uniformly over a surface are commonly called diapers—an expression supposed to be derived from Ypres, the name of the Flemish town where cloths so decorated were first or largely manufactured. They are composed of a repetition or series of the same ornament, in a vertical, horizontal, or a diagonal order. This is the most popular class of design for cotton-prints,

and the unit of repetition is generally small in these cases; but it may be either extremely simple, as a spot or star, in one colour, or as complicated and as rich as the diapers of the Alhambra, from which the mass of paper diapers are derived.

Diapers are suited for flat or round work of every class in manufactures or in mural decoration. Units of repetition, or repeats of irregular shapes, arranged diagonally, have the finest effects. A diaper, however, may be an alternation of two or more simple figures, just as it may be a constant repetition of one compound figure ; for as it is in this case the group that is repeated, the group of figures becomes the pattern or unit of repetition.

Geometric diapers are infinite, and by a judicious variation of colours may be made extremely beautiful. The majority of ancient mosaics are diapers of this character, and they are a good illustration of the carrying out of the principle of fitness in design ; for these geometric mosaics are nearly all floors, and they emphatically express *flatness*—an essential quality for a floor.

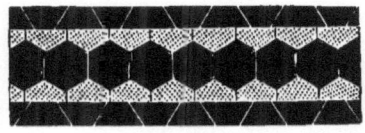

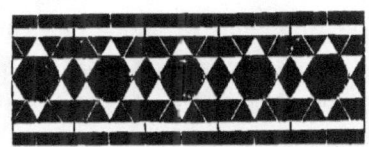

The diaper, then, is a uniform decoration of a surface : another general decoration analogous to it is a succession of stripes, of any character, or of colonnades. The colonnade consists of repetitions of continuous curves in the same direction : it is the favourite form of decoration for carpets, papers, lace, curtains, and some other textile manufactures : it is generally a decorated or foliated serpentine, and rarely a scroll—always a measured curved succession in vertical series.

All such superficial decoration is very simple : it is, in fact, as the paper-stainers expressively term it, mere *filling*, as it involves no scheming. You have but to design your repeat or unit of repetition ; the rest is mere mechanical expansion.

To uniformly cover a surface is, however, but the beginning of a designer's labours : his great business is to produce pleasing variety of surface, not only in the flat but in the round; not only upon regular but upon irregular surfaces.

The surface of a wall is of one kind; the surface of a sphere, a cylinder, or a cone, is of another. If we suppose a cylinder to represent the skeleton of a candlestick, it will not be sufficient to merely uniformly decorate the surface of this cylinder, and call it an ornamental candlestick. We must, in the first place, give the cylinder a shape which shall correspond with its destined use ; we must so balance the two ends that it will stand firmly upon one of them, and then, by varying the surface or form, give it a pleasing individuality of character consistent with its destination; and this is the process wherein the designer shows his skill. The principles applicable to one article may be quite the reverse of those applicable to another, and it is the designer's duty to suffer no mere ornamental predilections to interfere with the mechanical or practical excellence of his design. These are constant conditions far more important than those depending upon accidents of machinery. They are conditions of use, and it is these conditions by which a designer must primarily test his designs.

Taking it for granted that the eye requires variety of surface to gratify that faculty of the mind called taste, or to excite those emotions which we term *æsthetic*, how is this variety to be effected? By dividing surfaces into compartments, and by making some portions more prominent than others, and thus produce that contrast which we assumed at starting to be the element of all ornamental effects.

These compartments are known as panels, borders, cornice, frieze, basement or dado; capital, shaft, base, pedestal; neck, body, foot, and so on; all names designating the ornamental divisions of the general schemes of objects; though these things may not be ornamented, the mere division of an object into such parts is done for the sake of variety of effect, in obedience to one of the necessities of the mind.

These various compartments are separated or made prominent by mouldings: mouldings may be either mere suits of concave and convex members, as in many Gothic examples, or the concave series may be filled in with ornamental details. These may be plain or enriched mouldings; and, as boundaries of compartments, it is necessary that they should be particularly distinct, and we accordingly find that they are, in nearly all cases, the part of a design which has been most elaborated: call them edges or call them borders, the principle is the same throughout— whether the moulding of a room or piece of cabinet-work, the hem of a vest, the border of a shawl or handkerchief, the edge of a salver, we have everywhere the one principle of contrast in itself, and with its own ground.

As no border is introduced into a design for its own sake, but only as a contribution to the general effect, that is sure to be the best which is designed with a view to a principle rather than for any speciality of detail of its own: thus we find that a mere repeat, which shall contain an elemental principle, is superior to a prominent succession of elaborate and varied imitations, because special attraction to secondary details is not a merit, but a capital defect in a design. The border or moulding is the ornament, and not the details of which it is composed.

The truth of this principle is proved by the practice of all ages : we have not now to *create* Ornamental Art, but to *learn* it; it was established in all essentials long ago. As a proof of this I would instance the most popular decorations of the present day: we find that they are identical with the favourites of nearly all ages,—from Pericles to Pope Julius II., from Julius II. to the late King of Bavaria, Ludwig I.

CHAPTER IV.

WE still use the forms, and, indeed, the very details, adopted by the Greeks upwards of two thousand years ago. Why is this? Certainly not from their speciality of detail, but rather because it would be, perhaps, impossible to select others of a less decided individuality, which would so well illustrate the great principles of ornament,—series and contrast; contrast of masses, and contrast or harmony of lines. The details, however, will admit of every variation which will not disturb the order or arrangement on which the ornament depends: you may change the details to infinity, the ornament will remain the same as long as the arrangement is not disturbed. And this alternation is imperative if we wish to develop a rich and varied School of Ornamental Art.

The ornaments I refer to are,—the zigzag, the fret, the echinus, the astragal, the anthemions, the guilloche varieties, and the scrolls.

In the zigzag we have the simplest varieties of lines we can well conceive; in the frets we have a more complicated order of right-line series; in the varieties of the guilloche we have a similar simple series of curved lines or interlacings.

In the echinus, or what is commonly called the *egg and tongue*, we have another character, a bold alternation of light and shade; and we have a similar result on a smaller scale in the astragal: both belong essentially to the solid or *round*.

Echinus and Astragal. Erechtheium.

In the scrolls we have a regular running series of alternation of spirals, or any materials treated in that order of curve: use among the Romans has established an extraordinary prestige for the acanthus, but any other materials would answer the purpose.

In the anthemions we have a compound element, a succession or alternation of an harmonic group of curves, in a

Anthemion. Apollo Epicurius.

conventional adaptation of floral forms, as the name anthemion itself implies. In Greek examples we have a smaller and larger cluster alternated, sometimes reversed, sometimes enclosed in a curve, and generally connected by a band, by mere contact, or by some simple scroll.

Every example of an ornament must have an individuality of detail necessarily, but it is a great mistake to adopt this detail as an essential part of the ornament; for example, no two Greek anthemions are alike, but there are some few which contain a member a good deal resembling the honeysuckle: the ornament is simple and beautiful, but modern imitators overlooking its principle have comprehended only the detail, assumed it to be an imitation, and have called it the honeysuckle ornament. Instead, therefore, of grasping the source of a thousand ornaments equally beautiful, they have acquired but one, and half the classical buildings of modern times are covered with honeysuckles, bringing the whole art of Greece into disgrace for its monotony and formality, while there is scarcely a weed in England that might not with equal skill have been substituted for the honeysuckle, with perhaps equal effect, if only treated on the principle of a succession or alternation of an harmonic group of curves.

This is only one of the dilemmas that the designer must fall into by allowing mere specific details to usurp the place of the principles of ornament: his mind becomes occupied by a few individual forms, the very idea of principles is incomprehensible to him; and he necessarily remains a mere hack or imitator.

Where the mind views something more than the surface, or where the eyes are auxiliary only to the mind, every natural object may be suggestive of some new essential form or combination of forms. The lotus, the lily, and

E

the tulip, must be something more than flowers to the designer, or his use of them is limited indeed; each suggests distinct forms as applicable to various useful purposes.

All established styles of ornament are founded upon the same principles: their differences, which I shall in the following sketch endeavour to point out, are differences only of the materials, the details of the several favourite essential forms, which each more or less partially developed, some for one reason, some for another. The peculiarity of Egyptian and Byzantine ornament is owing to their prevailing symbolism, and certain details becoming standards: the peculiarity of the Saracenic is of exactly the opposite character, it scrupulously rejected everything approaching an individuality of detail; and accordingly the principles of ornament are perhaps more clearly developed in this style than in any other, because the details are so entirely subordinate.

We do not therefore admire the echinus and the astragal, because they are derived from the horse-chestnut or the huckle-bone, but because they are admirable details for that prominent contrast of light and shade which is so extremely valuable for edges or mouldings. It is the same with the whole series of popular ornaments; not one of them is beautiful because it represents any natural object, but because it has been chosen to illustrate certain symmetries or contrasts, by the very nature of vision delightful to the mind, just as harmonics and melodies delight it through another of its senses. I believe the analogy between music and ornament to be perfect: one is to the eye what the other is to the ear; and the day is not far distant when this will be practically demonstrated.

The principles of harmony, time or rhythm, and melody, are well defined in music, and indisputable: many men of many generations have devoted their entire lives to the development of these principles, and they are known. In ornament they are not known, and perhaps not recognised even as unknown quantities, because as yet no man has ever devoted himself to their elimination; though many ancient and middle-age designers have evidently had a true perception of them.

The first principle of ornament seems to be repetition. The simplest character of this is a measured succession, in series, of some one detail, as a moulding, for instance: this stage of ornament corresponds with melody in music, which is a measured succession of diatonic sounds, the system in both arising from the same source—rhythm—in music called also time, in ornament proportion or symmetry: proportion, or quantity, in both cases.

The second stage in music is harmony, or a combination of simultaneous sounds or melodies; it is also identical in ornamental art; every correct ornamental scheme is a combination of series, or measured succession of forms, and upon identical principles in music and ornament, called in the first counterpart, in the other symmetrical contrast.

Such a close analogy must convince us that ornament consists in something more than a mere artistic elaboration of either natural or conventional details, and that all mechanical ingenuity must be kept strictly subservient to theoretical principles of arrangement. The highest

mere imitative skill, employed on the most beautiful
natural materials, out of the strict province of so-called
fine art, will engender but mere fanciful vagaries, utterly
powerless on the eye as ornament, when compared with
even the crudest materials of the coarsest execution, if
only arranged in any order or combination of harmonic
progression.

Greek Terra Cotta.

CHARACTERISTICS OF STYLES.

CHAPTER V.

THE STYLES.

In a review of this kind, when we speak of the styles, we can comprise only the broad distinctions of ornament itself—the kinds or *genera*, not the mere specific varieties. There are, of course, many varieties of nearly every great style, but so long as the chief characteristics remain unchanged, the style is the same. From this point of view, therefore, the styles become comparatively few. We shall find that nine will comprise the whole number of the great characteristic developments which have had any influence on European civilisation, namely, three ancient—the Egyptian, the Greek, and the Roman; three medieval —the Byzantine, the Saracenic, and the Gothic; and three modern—the Renaissance, the Cinquecento, and the Louis Quatorze.

Several of these styles have their recognised varieties. Of the Greek there are the Doric and the Alexandrian; that is, the severe and the florid. Of the Byzantine, there are the Romanesque, Lombard, and Norman varieties, &c.; and of the Renaissance, also, there are several varieties. We speak of the Renaissance both as an epoch and as a style. As an epoch, it comprises many styles or varieties,

—the Trecento, the Cinquecento, the Renaissance (as a style, with its sub-varieties), the Elizabethan, the Louis XIV., the Louis XV., and the Rococo: the two last, however, are mere debased varieties of the Louis XIV., and they are decidedly the decay, not the revival, of art.

These various styles extend over a period of upwards of three thousand five hundred years, of which two thousand may be considered the ancient period, from the early historic times to the third century of our era. About one thousand years, from the third to the thirteenth century, may be considered the medieval period; and the last five centuries, from the thirteenth to the nineteenth, may be considered the period of the Renaissance, or the modern period.

Style is only another name for character. Every style, as such, depends, of course, upon what is *peculiar* to it, never on what it has in common with other styles. These peculiarities are what we term *characteristics*—the features by which it is distinguished.

Sometimes a style is merely a modification, or peculiar elaboration, of the features of another style. It is then only a variety or a derived style; and such varieties are common, especially in later times, the natural result of the accumulation of materials. These varieties the student will discover without aid, and, indeed, may invent at pleasure, when he is once master of the essential characteristics of the great historic styles.

As a matter of course, the earliest styles are the most simple, and, perhaps, necessarily also the most original, as each successive style has been gradually developed out of its predecessor,—as, the Roman from the. Greek, the

Romanesque from the Roman, and so on, with more or less affinity of character.

It does not follow, however, that an ornamental work is in a certain style because it belongs to the *period* of that style, for a style is defined not by its time or period, but by the prevailing peculiarities or characteristics of that period; and it is not at all the case that every work of a period possesses these peculiarities. It must be borne in mind, therefore, that while a genuine example of a style will always imply a certain time, a specimen of a certain time will only as a general rule illustrate the corresponding style. This is because no style is predetermined, but is, in its details, in all cases, incidental, notwithstanding a prevailing sentiment.

We will now then proceed to examine the nine great historic styles, which appear to sufficiently illustrate the history of ornament. The Egyptian, Greek, and Roman— the ancient; the Byzantine, Saracenic, the Gothic—the middle age; and the Renaissance, Cinquecento, and Louis Quatorze—the modern.

CHAPTER VI.

EGYPTIAN ORNAMENT.

ILLUSTRATED LITERATURE.

The works mentioned under this head are not cited as the authorities for the opinions given, as many of them were published some years after the preparation of the lectures, and the views do not always agree: they are referred to only as the most comprehensive or useful illustrated works on the subject, and as thus best adapted to aid the student in his labours.

EGYPT.—Description de l'Egypte, ou Recueil des Observations et des Recherches qui ont été faites en Egypte pendant l'Expédition de l'Armée Française. Publié par les ordres de sa Majesté l'Empereur Napoléon le Grand. (The great work of the French Expedition, treating of the Antiquities, Arts, Natural History, and Modern State of Egypt.) 23 vols. folio, atlas folio, and elephant. Paris, 1809, *et seq.*

---

* ANCIENT ART, 1848-49.
Syllabus.

LECTURE I.—ON THE DECORATIVE ART OF THE ANCIENT EGYPTIANS.

Early Establishment of Egyptian Art—about 1800 B.C. Its stationary and purely ornamental character. Extensive remains still preserved on the banks of the Nile, from Meroë to Alexandria, a distance of nearly 1200 miles.

Ipsambul, the Telamons. Essaboua, the Sphinx—Andro—Crio—and Hieraco-Sphinx. Philœ. Edfou, the Egyptian Temple—the Propyla, Obelisks, Mosaics, &c. Thebes, sumptuous Decoration of the Egyptian Temples — their Columns and Capitals. The Tombs. Denderah. Sakkara, the Arch. The Pyramids. Heliopolis. Egyptian style.

PORTER, SIR R. KER.—Travels in Georgia, Persia, Armenia, Ancient Babylonia, &c., during the years 1817, 1818, 1819, and 1820. 2 vols. 4to. London, 1821.

GAU, F. C.—Antiquités de la Nubie, ou Monumens inédits des Bords du Nil, situés entre la première et la seconde Cataracte, dessinés et mesurés en 1819. Ouvrage faisant suite au grand ouvrage de la Commission d'Egypte. Large folio. Paris, 1822.

RAM RAZ.—Essay on the Architecture of the Hindus. With 48 plates. 4to. London, 1834.

ROSELLINI, J.—The Monuments of Egypt and Nubia, arranged according to their subjects, by the Tuscan Expedition to Egypt, under the direction of Rosellini.

> I Monumenti dell' Egitto e della Nubia disegnati della spedizione scientifico-litteraria Toscana in Egitto : distribuiti in ordine di materie, interpretati ed illustrati dal Dottore Ippolito Rosellini. (This great work is in three parts, folio, with separate text in octavo. *Tavole* M. R. contains the Historical Monuments of the Kings, *Monumenti Storici*, in 169 plates: *Tavole* M. C. contains the Civil Monuments, *Monumenti Civili*, in 135 plates : *Tavole* M. D. C. the Monuments of Religious Worship, *Monumenti del Culto*, in 86 plates.) 3 vols. atlas folio, plates ; 9 vols. 8vo. text. Pisa, 1832-44.

LECTURE II.—EGYPT: ORNAMENTAL DETAILS.

Decorations of the Tombs. Painted Ceilings. Colours. Sunk-reliefs. Ornamental Types—the Zigzag, Labyrinth, Wave-scroll, Lotus, Winged-globe, Asp, and Cartouche. The Funerals. Manufactures—Furniture, Pottery, &c., Variegated Glass, Armour, Linen and Cotton Fabrics, Prints, Embroidered Stuffs. Ships, &c. Study of Ornament.

LECTURE III.—ASIA.

Egyptian and Asiatic Art characterised—Egyptian influence in Asia—Judæa, Assyria, India. Nimroud Marbles. Persepolis—Cambyses, Darius, Xerxes. The Ionian Greeks. General Similarity of Standard Ornamental Types in Ancient Monuments, whether Egyptian, Asiatic, or European.

LECTURE IV.—GREECE: HEROIC AGE OF GREEK ART.

Intercourse between Greece and Egypt. Greek Traditions. Legend of Origin of Greek Art—Dibutades of Corinth. Development of Painting —Skiagram, Polychrom, Monogram, and Monochrom—The Processes.

The Heroic Age of Greek Art, from about the 12th to the 8th century, B.C. inclusive. Pelasgic Remains—Mycenæ. Tomb of Agamemnon. The Greek Colonies in Asia Minor and Magna Græcia.

Development of Art as evinced in the Homeric Poems—Ornamental Armour, Toreutic Work, Embroidery, Woollen Fabrics of Miletus, Corinth, and Carthage. Shawl or Pallium of Alcisthenes of Sybaris. The Terra Cotta Vases.

Long, G.—The British Museum.—Egyptian Antiquities. 2 vols. 12mo. London, 1846.

Wilkinson, Sir J. G.—The Manners and Customs of the Ancient Egyptians, including their Private Life, Government, Laws, Arts, Manufactures, Religion, Agriculture, and Early History, derived from a Comparison of the Paintings, Sculptures, and Monuments still existing, with the Accounts of Ancient Authors. 3rd edition, 5 vols. 8vo. London, 1847.

Du Camp, M.—Egypte, Nubie, Palestine, et Syrie. Dessins photographiques, recueillis pendant les années 1849-50-51, et accompagnés d'un texte explicatif. 125 photographs, small folio. Paris, 1852-53.

Batissier, L.—Histoire de l'Art Monumental dans l'Antiquité, et au Moyen Age, suivie d'une Traité de la Peinture sur Verre. Imp. 8vo. Paris, 1845.

Layard, Dr. A. H.—The Monuments of Nineveh, from drawings made on the spot; illustrated in 100 plates. Folio. London, 1849.

LECTURE V.—GREECE: THE DORIC PERIOD—ORNAMENTAL ELEMENTS.—
THE GREEK ORDERS.

The Doric, or first Historic Age, from the 8th century to the 5th inclusive; from Cypselus of Corinth, and Rhœcus of Samos, to Pericles or Phidias.

The Doric Temples—Samos, Ægina, Pœstum, Athens. The Doric, the Echinus Order—the Parthenon, 438 B.C., the Temple of Apollo Epicurius. Ornamental details, painted and cut—the Zigzag, Fret or Labyrinth, Wave-scroll, Echinus, Astragal, Anthemion, or Palmette, the Polychromy.

The Ionic—the Voluted Order, prevalence of the Curve; the Volute and Guilloche or Speira—Chersiphron of Cnossus in Crete, 550 B.C. Temple of Diana at Ephesus.

The Corinthian—the Acanthus Order. Callimachus of Corinth, about 400 B.C.

Greek and Egyptian Temple compared—the Pediment or Eagle, the Frieze or Zophoros—Image-bearer, Caryatides, Canephoroe.

LECTURE VI.—GREECE: PERIOD OF ALEXANDER. ASIATIC INFLUENCE—
THE DECLINE.

Complete Establishment of Greek Art at the time of Alexander the Great, 336 B.C. The Three Styles at Athens—the Parthenon, 438 B.C.; the Erechtheium, 409 B.C.; the Choragic Monument of Lysicrates, 335 B.C.

The Mural Decorations—the Lesche at Delphi, the Poëcile at Athens; Polygnotus, Zeuxis, Apelles.

Statue Painting. Chryselephantine Sculpture—the Olympian Jupiter, 433 B.C. Phidias.

Elements of Greek Art conventional, and purely æsthetic—the Myths—Sphinx, Chimæra, Griffin, Satyr, &c.—Orientalization of Greek taste—Alexander, his Influence, his Funeral, 321 B.C. The Potteries of Samos, Athens, and Etruria.

LAYARD, DR. A. H.—A second series of the Monuments of Nineveh, including bas-reliefs from the Palace of Sennacherib, and Bronzes from the ruins of Nimroud, from drawings made on the spot during a Second Expedition to Assyria. 71 plates, oblong folio. London, 1853.

FERGUSSON, J.—Illustrations of the Rock-cut Temples of India. Fol. London, 1834.

———— The Palaces of Nineveh and Persepolis Restored: an Essay on Ancient Assyrian and Persian Architecture. 8vo. London, 1851.

———— Picturesque Illustrations of Ancient Architecture in Hindostan. Folio. London, 1852.

———— The Illustrated Handbook of Architecture; being a concise and popular account of the different styles of architecture prevailing in all ages, and in all countries. With 850 woodcuts. Folio. London, 1857.

JONES, O.—The Grammar of Ornament. Drawn on stone by F. Bedford. Folio. London, 1856-8.

(On the styles generally.)

THE earliest style of ornament of which we know anything of material importance is the Egyptian, dating from about

---

1800 B.C., when it was already completely established; and this is literally a hieroglyphic style in its sentiments and in its details; both are derived from a priestly symbolism. As a rule, the elements of Egyptian ornament have a particular meaning; they are not often, if ever, arbitrarily chosen for the sake of beauty of effect. The style is accordingly, though abounding in materials, very simple and limited in its arrangements, in comparison with

Ruins at Thebes.

later styles, in which mere symbolism was superseded by the pure æsthetic principles of art; that is, *effect*, not *meaning*, being the object of the artist. Yet we cannot but admire the ingenuity with which the Egyptian decorator, by a mere symmetrical arrangement, has converted even the incomprehensible hieroglyphics into pleasing and tasteful ornaments. A simple symmetrical arrangement, however, is the limit of his artistic scheming, and generally in the shape of a simple progression, whether in a horizontal line or repeated on the principle of the diaper, that is, row upon row, horizontally or diagonally. The painted ceilings of the Tombs of the Kings at Thebes afford many good examples.

In one class of ornament Egypt is eminent, independent of its skilful application of art to manufactures: it is eminent in its complete adaptation of its own natural productions in the development of a style peculiar to itself, in its conventional treatment of local natural types, as, for instance, the lotus or water-lily of the Nile, the element of so many varieties of ornament. The Egyptian details are not mere crude imitations of nature, but natural objects, selected by symbolism, and fashioned by symmetry into ornamental decorations. So that we have here one great class of ornament, and the earliest systematic efforts in design in the world's history. Many of the details of the Egyptians are still popular ornaments, handed down by successive ages to our own time.

When we consider the heirarchical vassalage of the Egyptian artist, and that he was by birth, and not by choice, in his profession—as every man, by the law of caste, was forced to pursue the occupation of his father, in spite of his tastes or capabilities—we must admit that he displays peculiar ability. In many respects, the art was as thoroughly understood at Memphis or Thebes three thousand years ago as it is at London or Paris this day. The shapes of the Egyptian ewer and basin, and other vessels for domestic purposes, are identical with those of the most favourite patterns of the present time; and many Egyptian ornaments are still popular ornaments, and have been so through all times; as the fret or labyrinth, wave-scroll, spiral, zigzag, water-lily, star, and palm. They had many others derived from the vegetable productions of Egypt.

In the first place, Egyptian ornament admits of no pictures of objects; all are treated conventionally. Even in the wall-paintings themselves, no object is fairly painted as it actually appears; the best examples are but intelligible representations—mere elevations or dia-grams.

The arrangements are almost exclusively a mere sym-metrical series or progression, and always of a very simple order; but precious stones and metals, and the richest materials generally, seem to have been very abundantly used. The frieze or broad-band is the commonest form of these decorations; and the details are generally some of the more important symbols, as the lotus, or water-lily of the Nile, the type of its inundations, from which Egypt derives its fruitfulness, and the zigzag, the type of water or the Nile itself. This ancient signification of the zigzag is still preserved in the present zodiac sign of the Water-carrier, or Aquarius. The fret or labyrinth, another right-line series and important symbol, is of less frequent occur-rence.

There is, however, one particular ornament which is more common than all others in Egyptian decoration. This is what is sometimes called the Scarabæus or beetle, or, rather, the Winged-globe; it occurs of all sizes and almost in all materials, and is a species of

talisman or invocation of good luck (Agathodæmon).
The globe is supposed to represent the sun, the wings
providence, and the two asps, one on each side of the
globe, dominion or monarchy; the creative, protective,
and distributive powers, implying *order*, the κοσμος, or
world, of the Greeks.

We almost invariably find this ornament placed over
doors, windows, and in passages, and sometimes of an
enormous size, extending thirty feet or more. It is also
frequent in costume, and on the mummy-cases. There
are several other winged figures found in Egyptian friezes,
natural and conventional, as the vulture with the tau and
ostrich feather, the hawk, the winged asp, and the human
winged figure, corresponding apparently to those described
in the works of the Jews.

The sphinx, a remarkable object in Egyptian art, does
not come under the category of the winged creatures.
In this it is distinguished from the Greek creation of
that name, which is always winged, and always female.
The Egyptian sphinx, on the other hand, is always
male. It is supposed to represent the combination of
physical and intellectual power, or the kings, as incarna-
tions of such attributes. They are also associated with
the special forms and attributes of the great Egyptian
deities, Osiris and Ammon, Neph or Jupiter, and Phreh
or Helios: that is, we have the Man-sphinx, the Ram-
sphinx, and the Hawk-sphinx, or the lion's body with the
head of the man, the ram, or the hawk, according to the
deity worshipped. These sphinxes were thus named by
the Greeks respectively the Andro-sphinx, the Crio-sphinx,
and the Hieraco-sphinx. The principal position of the

sphinx was on either side of the dromos, or path, leading to the temple.

The swelling asp alone (the Cobra de capello) is also a very characteristic ornament. We find entire friezes and borders composed of a mere succession of these asps, and it is very common to find them arranged also in symmetrical opposition, one on each side of the cartouche or shield, enclosing the hieroglyphic name of a king, having the same signification of dominion, with a special reference to the king or dynasty expressed by the hieroglyphic in the cartouche.

The most essential symbolic characteristics of an Egyptian design, then, are these—the winged globe, the lotus and the papyrus, the zigzag, the asp, and the cartouche containing hieroglyphics. The lotus is, perhaps, the most common. These we find mixed up with many arbitrary or geometrical forms, as the fret, spiral or wave-scroll, star, &c., and with any of the natural productions of Egypt, conventionally treated, and in simple symmetrical progression; every detail, probably, having a symbolic meaning beyond its mere ornamental service in the design.

The fret, perhaps, may be enumerated, among the more important symbols, as the type of the labyrinth of Lake Mœris, with its twelve palaces and three thousand chambers, indicating, in their turn, the twelve signs of the zodiac, and the three thousand years of transmigrations which the wandering soul is condemned to undergo. The wave-scroll, also, may represent water in motion, or the waves. Its name was derived from its form. Our designation is but a translation of the Greek Cyma or the Roman

Cymatium. Minor symbols, as among the hieroglyphics, are found in endless variety in costume and in ordinary decoration. For these, the student may refer to the works of Rosellini and of Wilkinson.

Gaudy diapers and general gaiety of colour are likewise characteristic of Egyptian taste, but the colours are generally limited to red, blue, yellow, and green, though the Egyptians were acquainted with nearly all other colours. I have mentioned a simple progression or repetition as characteristic of the Egyptian style; and it is certainly very rarely that we find anything more, yet, in the cluster of the Lotus, in the form of its leaf, we have a very beautiful compound example, a symmetrical arrangement of the flower in a circular, or rather oval series, constituting the unit of the ordinary horizontal series.* And this ornament is important, as anticipating the anthemion or most popular floral ornament of the Greeks, so common in architecture and in the terra-cotta vases. The Egyptians, however, antici-

Temple at Denderah.

---

* It is found painted on a palanquin in a picture in the Tombs of the Kings, and is not unlike a series of the hats of the God Nilus, with its seven drooping lilies.

pated the Greeks in something more than some ordinary details. Their temples display a great diversity of pillars, from the mere fluted columns of Beni Hassan to the gorgeous varieties of Thebes, Philæ, and Denderah.

But although the Egyptians, except in the case of the Isis capital, as well shown at Denderah, systematically varied their pillars in the same colonnades, two alike with their decorations complete never being placed together, except as a pair of opposites, their varieties may be reduced to three essential forms—the truncated lotus-bud, the lotus-bell, and the Isis head. Every capital is a variety of one of these essential forms; but the lotus or papyrus-bell of the middle period is much the most common. The abacus is, on all occasions, the width only of

Ruins at Philæ.

the pillar, and invariably narrower than the capital, which is a valuable feature, and very essential to the effect of stability. The Egyptian pillars vary in their altitudes from about four to nearly seven diameters, the longer proportions being the most common.

The general massiveness of Egyptian architecture, though, when transported to other climates, it may appear heavy, is particularly appropriate to the climate and landscape of Egypt itself.

The various altitudes and horizontal masses of the great divisions of an Egyptian temple, as still seen at Philæ and elsewhere breaking with their bold shadows the dazzling undulating mass of light characterising the general landscape, are calculated in the highest degree to give delight and repose to the eye in their general features, while the gay polychromic decorations of their surfaces constitute a rich centre of attraction, modifying the excessive brilliancy of the surrounding scene.

The Egyptian style of decoration was not without its influence upon all people connected with Egypt; on the Jews, on the Greeks, and more especially on the Persians after the plunder of Thebes by Cambyses, who, Diodorus Siculus informs us, carried away a colony of Egyptian artists back into Persia: and we still see the remains of their influence in the whole basin of the Euphrates and on the borders of the Persian Gulf, from Nineveh to Persepolis. The so-called Nineveh sculptures recently deposited in the British Museum are identical in style with those of Persepolis, the work of this Egyptian colony, according to Diodorus, introduced by Cambyses in the latter part of the sixth century before our era ; but the works were chiefly carried out under the direction of his successors, Darius and Xerxes. Independent of this tradition, there is considerable evidence of Egyptian influence in the works themselves. The winged figure of Cyrus at Mourgab or Pasargadæ has a decided Egyptian character, and the head-dress appears to be that of the Egyptian god Malooli, a son of Isis and Horus. The change in the general character of the sculpture may be explained by the fact that the Egyptians worked in Persia under the influence of the Persian priesthood instead of their own. The subject bull, which figures largely in the Persepolitan sculptures, is explained as signifying the overthrow of the Assyrian power by the Persian. The Persepolitan, like the Assyrian sculptures, are inscribed with the arrow-headed characters.

The name of Sennacherib, who was murdered by his own son in 711, is the oldest name yet discovered in the inscriptions; and as his achievements in Judæa, in 713, are recorded, the oldest sculptures are since his time, or, at the earliest, in the seventh century before our era. Unless much later works, they must, however, belong to the seventh century before our era; but the ruins are found in three distinct places—Khorsabad, Kouyunjik, and Nimroud, apparently much too remote from each other ever to have constituted a single city. The so-called north-west palace, that of Nimroud, is supposed to have been built by Ninus II. and Sardanapalus (Esarhaddon) III.; Kouyunjik, by an earlier Sardanapalus.

The entire city was destroyed by Nabopolassar, the father of Nebuchadnezzar, in 606, and the same king destroyed Jerusalem in 588; he rebuilt Babylon, which was, in its turn, destroyed by Cyrus in 538 B.C.

Darius Hystaspes, who succeeded Cambyses in 521 B.C., had been with that king in Egypt, as one of his body-

Sacred Tree. Assyrian Marbles, British Museum.

guard, and he was apparently the real builder of Persepolis and of the palace of Susa.   He is, perhaps, the
most distinguished of the Asiatic sovereigns for his
architectural undertakings.   He carried on extensive
works in Egypt, rebuilt the Temple of Jerusalem in 514,
and made himself a summer palace at Ecbatana.   May
he not have extended his love of repairs as far also as
Nineveh ?   The arrow-headed inscriptions are also at
Persepolis (it is a mode of writing persevered in to much
later times), and some of the singular figures at Nineveh
are found also on Darius's own tomb at Nakshi Rustam.
The difference of dialect on the inscriptions would be
explained by their being written by different people,
without any necessity for the supposition of a difference
of time.   The subject of a series of sculptures must set
a limit to their antiquity, but cannot otherwise fix their
time.   However, as the assumed works of Nineveh
perished with the city nearly a century before the
execution of the works of Persepolis, these last cannot
have been copied from those of Nineveh,—in the time
of Darius a remote heap, probably, of unknown or for-
gotten ruins.

   It is hazardous to venture an opinion upon the period
of works which, to all appearance, have their history
inscribed on them, because these inscriptions, when
interpreted, may prove a very authentic contradiction
to the opinion ventured; but according to our tests of
characteristics of style, the sculptures lately brought
from the neighbourhood of Ancient Nineveh (or Calah)
are certainly of the same school as those of Persepolis,
if not of the same time.

In Egypt, we found grandeur of proportion, simplicity of parts, and splendour or costliness of material—gold, silver, and ivory, precious stones, and colour—as the great art characteristics. And we find throughout, that the prevailing characteristic of Asiatic art, also, is sumptuousness. It is equally displayed in the works of the Tabernacle, in the Temple of Solomon, in the buildings of Semiramis and of Nebuchadnezzar at Babylon, and in the palaces of the Persian kings.

Jewish ornament, like the Egyptian, appears to have been purely representative. The only elements mentioned in Scripture are the almond, the pomegranate, the palm-tree, the lily or lotus, oxen, lions, and the cherubim. The only example we possess of Jewish ornamental work is the bas-relief of the candlestick of seven branches, still partly preserved among the sculptures of the Arch of Titus at Rome. Extending our view still farther east, we find the most characteristic feature of Hindoo art seems to be the fantastic; and though possessing the same jewelled richness as the Egyptian, it wants its simplicity and grandeur. Its most striking peculiarities are its fantastic animal devices, and a profusion of minute foliage. But I believe most Indian work to be modern compared with Egyptian.*

It is not till we come to Greece that we find the habitual introduction of forms for their own sake, or for their æsthetic value or effect, purely as ornaments; and this is a very great step in art.

* On the Rules and Proportions of Hindoo Architecture, see Ram Raz.

CHAPTER VII.

GREEK ORNAMENT.

ILLUSTRATED LITERATURE.

IONIAN ANTIQUITIES, published, with permission of the Society of Dillettanti, by R. Chandler, M.A., N. Revett, architect, and W. Pars, painter. Folio. London, 1769.

PAOLI, P. A.—Ruins of Pæstum.
Rovine della Citta di Pesto detta ancora Posidonia. Folio. Rome, 1784.

HAMILTON, SIR W.—Collection of Engravings from Ancient Vases, mostly of Pure Greek workmanship, discovered in Sepulchres in the Kingdom of the Two Sicilies, but chiefly in the neighbourhood of Naples, during the course of the years 1789-90, now in the possession of Sir W. Hamilton ; wi h remarks on each Vase by the Collector. 3 vols. large 4to. Naples, 1791-95.

STUART AND REVETT.—The Antiquities of Athens measured and delineated. 4 vols. folio. London, 1762-1816.

———— Supplement to the above by Cockerell, Kinnard, Donaldson, Jenkins, and Railton. Folio. London, 1830.

BRITISH MUSEUM.—A Description of the Collection of Ancient Marbles in the British Museum, with engravings, chiefly from drawings by H. Corbould. 10 vols. 4to. London, 1812, *et seq.*

DE QUINCY, Q.—Le Jupiter Olympien, ou l'Art de la Sculpture Antique considérée sous un nouveau point de vue, &c. (The mode of constructing the Chryselephantine works considered.) Folio. Paris, 1815.

———— Monuments et Ouvrages d'Art Antiques, resti ués d'après les Descriptions des Ecrivains Grecs et Latins, et accompagnés de Dissertations Archéologiques. (Attempted restorations in coloured plates of Chryselephantine and other celebrated works of Ancient Art.) 2 vols. 4to. Paris, 1829.

MILLENGEN, J.—Ancient Unedited Monuments. Pai ted Greek Vases, from collections in various countries, principally in Great Britain, illustrated and explained. 4to. London, 1822.

II

VULLIAMY, L.—Examples of Ornamental Sculpture in Architecture. Drawn from the Original of Bronze, Marble, and Terra Cotta, in Greece, Asia Minor, and Italy, in the years 1818-19-20-21. 2nd edition, 4to. London, *n. d.*

BOUILLON AND ST. VICTOR.—The Ancient Marbles in the Louvre. Musée des Antiques, dessiné et gravé par P. Bouillon, Peintre, avec des Notices explicatives par J. B. de St. Victor. 3 vols. folio. Paris, 1821-27.

NORMAND, C.—Nouveau Parallèle des Ordres d'Architecture des Grecs, des Romains, et des Auteurs modernes. Folio. Paris, 1828.

MICALI, G.—Monuments illustrating the History of the Ancient People of Italy. Monumenti per servire alla Storia degli Antichi Popoli Italiani; raccolti esposti, e pubblicati da Giuseppe Micali. Small folio. Florence, 1832. Text, 4 vols. 8vo. 1832-44.

PENROSE.—An Investigation of the Principles of Athenian Architecture, or the results of a recent survey, conducted chiefly with reference to the optical refinements exhibited in the construction of the ancient buildings at Athens. Illustrated by numerous engravings. (Published by the Society of Dillettanti.) Folio. London, 1851.

HITTORFF, J. J.—On Greek Polychromy, or the Painting of Architecture. Restitution du Temple d'Empédocle à Sélinonte, ou l'Architecture Polychrome chez les Grecs. Text, 4to.; plates, atlas folio. Paris, 1851.

WEITBRECHT, C. — Ornamenten Zeichnungs-Schule. (Ornamental Drawing-School for Artists, Manufacturers, and Workmen.) 100 plates. 2nd edition. Oblong folio. Stuttgart, 1852.

BÖTTICHER, KARL VON.—The Art of the Greeks in its relation to the Beautiful in Architecture, and in the Industrial Arts. Die Tektonik der Hellenen. Text, 2 vols. 4to.; atlas of plates, 2 vols. folio. Potsdam, 1852-53.

HOLZ, F. W.—Details of the principal Greek Mouldings. Details Greichischer Haupt-Gesimse zusammengestellt für die mannigfachsten Anwendungen, in 40 blättern. 4to. Berlin, 1854.

DONALDSON, T. L.—Architectura Numismatica, or Architectural Medals of Classic Antiquity. Illustrated and explained by comparison with the monuments and the description of ancient authors, and copious text. Imp. 8vo. London, 1859.

———

THE next great historic style we have to review is the Greek. First we must speak of the Doric, or early Greek, which comprises the Etruscan—evidently derived

from it; and we find no less a change in the general
character than in the details in this first European style,
when compared with the art of Egypt or of Asia. Art
becomes now for the first time purely æsthetic.

It is, in fact, to the substitution of the æsthetic
principle in the place of the symbolic, rather than to

Antefix of the Parthenon.

variety of element, that we have a new development of
taste in the art of the Greeks. It is this, also, which
constitutes its originality; its technical processes were
perhaps, in the early stages, identical with the Egyptian.
With the great commerce and intimate intercourse which
were established between Greece and Egypt in the

seventh century, and perhaps earlier, it is impossible but that the Greeks were sufficiently acquainted with all the arts of the Egyptians, and that very much was learned by them from the Egyptians, although, in the great cities, the traditionary records or later versions of records generally claim the art as indigenous and original. The traditions, however, of less important localities, as occasionally repeated by Pausanias, carry the whole evidence to the other side of the question. The arts of the Greeks appear to have been established much earlier, or more extensively, in the islands, and especially at Samos, than in Greece itself.

The Doric age—the first historic age of Greek art—comprises altogether a period of about four centuries from the first historic records; from Rhœcus of Samos and Cypselus of Corinth, until Phidias and Pericles and their immediate successors. The previous period from the traditions of the Trojan war, belongs rather to what may be termed the heroic age. The style of this period extended from the Western shores of Asia to the extreme limits of Sicily, as shown in the many interesting Doric ruins still preserved. The most important manufacture of the period of which remains exist, was that of the terra-cotta vases; and on these we find all the characteristic ornaments of the distinctively Greek style of decoration. We find on these vases exactly the same ornaments, but necessarily modified in their treatment, as those which distinguished the architectural monuments of the time.

There are two classes of the painted Greek pottery, the black and the yellow; that is, those which have

From Treasury or Tomb at Mycenæ, Argolis. British Museum.

Erechtheium, Athens. British Museum.

Example of Fret or Labyrinth.

Anthemion. Apollo Epicurius.

Echinus and Astragal. Erechtheium.

Example of Guilloche.

black figures and ornaments, the ground of the vase
being left the colour of the clay; and those which have
the ground painted black, and the figures left the colour
of the clay. Of the black or former class there are two
varieties, the one painted only with animals, the other
with figures, &c. The earliest belong to the date of
about 600 B.C.; the second may be generally reckoned
as a century later. Of the yellow vases there are three
varieties or sub-classes—the severe, the beautiful, and
the rich, so called from the various characters of their
decorations; and these belong respectively to the general
dates 400, 300, and 200, B.C., when the manufacture
seems to have ceased. There are two other kinds of
vases which, in an ornamental view, may be considered
to commence and to terminate the series; those that are
not painted, but are merely decorated with zigzags and
frets in a manner resembling wicker-work; and those
which are painted with the complete encaustic picture
in all colours. The last are very rare, and belong to
the latest date, about 200 B.C.; the first are even older
than the most ancient black vases, and may be considered
as belonging to the seventh century before our era.

The first ornaments which attract our notice on these
vases, of all periods, are those with which we have already
become familiar in Egyptian art—the zigzag, the wave-
scroll, and the labyrinth, or Greek fret. But perhaps the
most characteristic ornaments of the period are the
echinus, or horse-chestnut (egg and tongue), and the
anthemion, commonly known in its most simple form as
the honeysuckle or palmette, both of which it somewhat
resembles, as represented in the Doric antefixes. But

the anthemion, or flower-ornament, is more than the mere honeysuckle (or palm-branch, whatever it may be), even when so applied: it is this flower-form alternated with the lily or analogous form. This is the case with every example, except a very few, upon the vases. There is, however, no actual imitation whatever in Greek ornamental art. Occasionally, also, in this period emblematic ornaments were used which referred to the mysteries, sacrifices, funeral rites, and the games; but instances are not frequent. At all events, such ornaments do not belong to prominent characteristics of style.

The architectural features of the Greek are still more distinctive than the ornamental in comparison with the Egyptian. The flat, ponderous, sloping buildings of the Egyptians are both beautiful and useful in the landscape and climate of Egypt; and just as the rainless heat of Egypt developed the massive flat roofs, so the rainy seasons of Greece rendered the sloping roof necessary, the gable of which the Greeks eventually developed into their beautiful pediment. The pediment seems to have necessitated another member in the entablature, the frieze; a feature æsthetically more than mechanically necessary to diminish the apparent weight of the pediment, to balance the parts, and to strengthen, in effect, the entablature. The only Greek example of a temple without a pediment—the Pandroseium at Athens—has no frieze in its entablature.

The distinctive ornament of the three Greek architectural orders, as they are termed, is the capital. The Doric capital consists of a round flat cushion, called the echinus, and a large square abacus, the lower diameter of the echinus being that of the pillar, its upper that of the abacus. The cushion is called the echinus, from its being invariably decorated (painted) with that ornament. As this ornament is so constant, the Doric order may be descriptively termed the *echinus order;* and the echinus is accordingly the principal ornament of the period.

Like the Egyptian, the Greek is distinguished for its broad, flat surfaces. Even its curves are flat, of a parabolic character; a development, perhaps, due to the practice of polychromic decoration. Everything was coloured; and high relief, as producing shadows, is antagonistic to the display of colour.

In a general classification we may combine the Doric and Alexandrian as one style, the Greek, unless we wish to distinguish between early and late Greek; and as they really are distinct, it is proper to separate their characteristics here; but of course the second comprises the first.

Of the early period, then, to recapitulate, the characteristic features are—the echinus, the wave-scroll (sometimes called the Vitruvian scroll), the fret or labyrinth, the zigzag, the anthemion, and occasionally the astragal; and the terra-cotta vases have given such a prestige to black and tawny yellow that their combination has become a characteristic colouring—not, however, to the exclusion of red, blue, yellow, green, or white. Purple and saffron may likewise be said to be characteristic of this period, as the favourite colours for male and female costume.

On the whole, foliage performs a very secondary part in the ornamentation of this age. We have conventional floriage more prominent; and we have comparatively a great variety of geometrical forms and combinations in the diapers and their borders, found roughly indicated in the dresses on the vases.

The second Greek period, which may be called the Alexandrian, although Alexander does not strictly mark it—for it may be said to begin with the Erechtheium at Athens, 409 B.C.—enriched all these forms, and made some more familiar, as the astragal or huckle-bone series; and it added to them the spiral; the guilloche, or speira (plat); the acanthus; and, in a very simple development, the ordinary scroll, consisting of a succession of spirals reversed alternately. It further established the practice of *carving* the ornaments, instead of merely *painting* them, as was the prevailing custom in the Doric period. The Ionic capital has now supplanted the Doric; and the horns, or volutes, are added to the echinus, the characteristic ornament of the Doric capital.

From the Temple of Diana at Daphne.

The first of these two styles was magnificently displayed by the Parthenon at Athens, 438 B.C. The second was best exhibited in the Ionic temples of Asia Minor; but it is also very completely represented in the Erechtheium; and in a third order, the acanthus, called historically the

Corinthian order, in the choragic monument of Lysicrates at Athens, 335 B.C. Both are well illustrated by the Elgin Room in the British Museum, where are specimens from these and other Greek monuments.

The Ionic, or voluted echinus capital, is attributed to Chersiphron of Cnossus, in Crete; and though occurring comparatively late in Greece, as even the Doric order itself, it was established in Asia Minor as early as the middle of the sixth century before our era, as the great Ionic pillars of the Temple of Diana at Ephesus—one of the seven wonders of the world—were executed at the expense of Crœsus, King of Lydia, who died 546 B.C.

The acanthus capital is called "Corinthian," from its reputed discovery by Callimachus of Corinth, who lived about 400 B.C.

After the establishment of the Ionic order, in which the volute is so prominent, we find the curved line, as the element of the guilloches, more common, in some degree supplanting the fret, or right-lined plat; the curved-line ornament being palpably more in harmony with the volute. This is another example of that propriety of taste in Greek art which is also illustrated in the common juxtaposition of the astragal with the echinus. The ordinary scroll and acanthus are kept subdued in Greek work in comparison with the echinus, anthemion, and others; and, in the sense in which we use the term, they are much more *characteristic* of Roman than of Greek art.

It is the same with the three great classic orders—all three Greek by origin; but the acanthus order was very little used by the Greeks, while with the Romans it was the favourite. As regards style, therefore, it is more

I

characteristic of the Roman than the Greek. The only Greek scroll worthy of the name is the very simple one of the roof of the choragic monument of Lysicrates.

The most simple form of the scroll is of very rare occurrence, even on the painted terra-cotta vases; but it is not uncommon on the ordinary red ware of the Romans, and in these examples it has preserved its Greek character. There is always a great simplicity both in the details and in the arrangement of the materials of Greek ornament: it is generally the various elements arranged in simple horizontal series, one row above the other.

Ancient Bronze Lamp, found in the Thames.

CHAPTER VIII.

ROMAN ORNAMENT.

ILLUSTRATED LITERATURE.

PIRANESI, G. AND F.—Greek and Roman Antiquities, Paintings, &c. 29 vols. fol. Paris, 1835-7.

WOOD AND DAWKINS.—The Ruins of Palmyra, otherwise Tedmor in the Desert. Folio. London, 1753.

——— The Ruins of Balbec, otherwise Heliopolis, in Cœlosyria. Folio. London, 1757.

MOREAU, C.—Fragmens et Ornemens d'Architecture, dessinés à Rome d'après l'antique. Folio. Paris, 1800.

TATHAM, C. H.—Etchings, representing the best Examples of Ancient Ornamental Architecture, drawn from the originals in Rome, and other parts of Italy, during the years 1794, 1795, and 1796. 3rd edition, small folio. London, 1810.

ROME.—The most remarkable Buildings of Ancient Rome.
Raccolta delle più insigni Fabbriche di Roma Antica e sue adjacenze. Misurate Nuovamente e dichiarate dall' Architetto Giuseppe Valadier, illustrate con osservazioni antiquarie da Filippo Aurelio Visconti, ed incise da Vincenzo Feoli. Folio. Roma, 1810-22.

WILKINS, W.—The Civil Architecture of Vitruvius, comprising those Books of the Author which relate to the Public and Private Edifices of the Ancients. Illustrated by numerous engravings. With an Introduction, containing an Historical View of the Rise and Progress of Architecture among the Greeks. Folio. London, 1812.

MAZOIS, F.—Les Ruines de Pompéi, dessinées et mesurées par F. Mazois, pendant les années 1809, 1810, 1811.
Ouvrage continué par M. Gau, précédé d'une notice sur F. Mazois par M. le Chevalier Artaud, et de l'explication de la grande Mosaïque découverte à Pompéi en 1831, par M. Quatremère de Quincy. Le texte de la quatrième partie a été rédigé par M. Barré. 4 vols. folio. Paris, 1812-38.

TAYLOR AND CRESY.—The Architectural Antiquities of Rome. 2 vols. folio. London, 1821.

GELL AND GANDY.—Pompeiana : the Topography, Edifices, and Ornaments of Pompeii. 4 vols. imperial 8vo. London, 1824-32.

CANINA, L.—Ancient Architecture, explained by its Monuments: Greek, Roman, &c. L'Architettura antica descritta e demonstrata coi Monumenti. Text, 9 vols. 8vo. Plates, 4 vols. folio. Roma, 1834-46.

ALBERTOLLI, FERD.—Friezes from the Forum of Trajan, with others in Rome, and various other cities.

> Fregi trovati negli scavi del Foro Trajano, con altri esistenti in Roma ed in diverse altre città; disegnati e misurati sul luogo da Ferdinando Albertolli. Folio. Milan, 1838.

ZAHN, W.—The most beautiful Ornaments and most remarkable Paintings of Pompeii, Herculaneum, and Stabiæ, &c., from original drawings made on the spot.

> Die schönsten Ornamente und merkwürdigsten Gemälde aus Pompeii, Herkulanum, und Stabiæ, nebst einigen Grundrissen und Ansichten, nach den an Ort und Stelle gemachten Originalzeichnungen, von Wilhelm Zahn. Folio. Berlin, 1829-54, *et seq*.

———— Ornaments of all Classic Art Epochs, represented from the originals in their proper colours.

> Ornamente aller Klassischen Kunst Epochen nach den originalen in ihren eigenthümlichen farben dargestellt. Oblong folio. Berlin, 1849.

WIESELER, F.—Theatres, &c., of the Greeks and Romans.

> Theatergebäude und Denkmäler des Bühnenwesens bei den Griechen und Römern. 4to. Göttingen, 1851.

WE come now to the third and last ancient style, the Roman. In this, however, we have simply an enlargement or enrichment of the florid Greek. It did not add a single important element to the Greek, but elaborated the established elements with every possible variety of effect, and with all the exuberance and richness of which they are capable, developing some into comparatively colossal proportions. It was, therefore, original only in its treatment of the Greek materials. Roman art is accordingly still Greek art; and it is more than probable

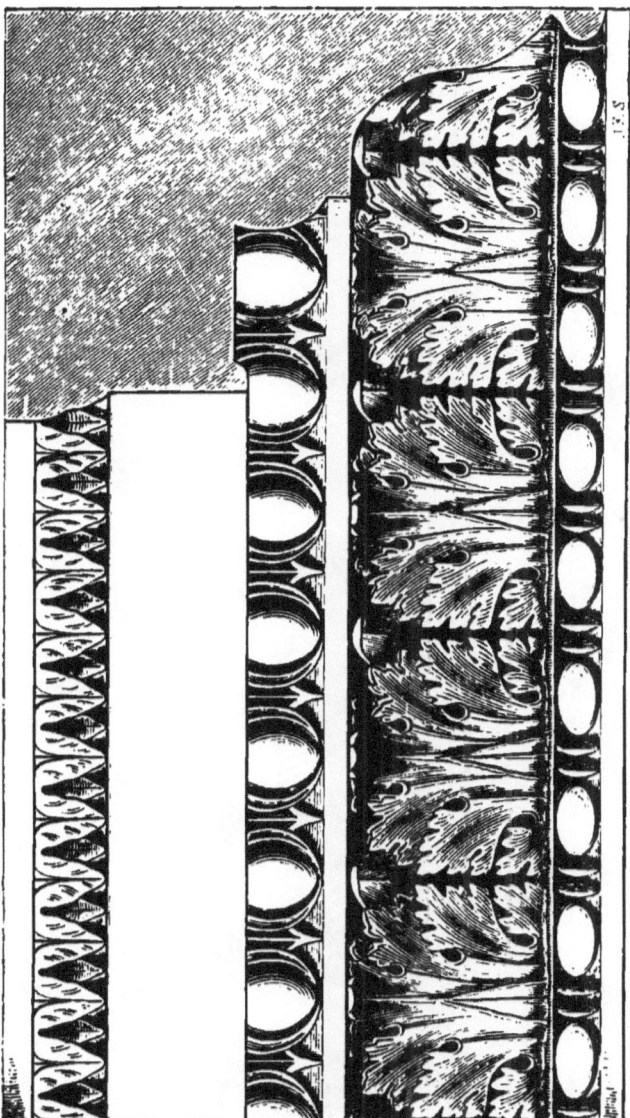

Cornice of Pedestal, Trajan's Column, Rome.

Echinus and Astragal.　Pantheon, Rome.

Jupiter Tonans, Rome.

　Jupiter Stator, Rome.

Olive Acanthus. Mars Ultor, Rome.

Nest of Scroll. Ancient Panel, Florence.

that nearly all the great artists employed by the Romans were Greeks, not only in the provinces, as at Petra, Palmyra, Baalbec, or at Athens (Temple of Jupiter), Pola, and Spalatro, but at Rome itself, where the most magnificent Forum, that of Trajan, was the work of a Greek.

However, though not original, Roman ornament has its peculiar characteristics, as well as every other style. The chief of these is its uniform magnificence. The most simple Greek ornament becomes, under Roman treatment, if not a magnificent, at least an elaborate decoration. In fact, the most florid Greek example, as the choragic monument of Lysicrates for instance, becomes a very simple design in comparison with only an ordinary Roman specimen.

The architectural orders, though preserved in nearly their pure Greek form also, have not escaped this enrichment; and the composite, the only distinct Roman order, comprises, as its name literally implies, all the three Greek orders at once—the echinus, the voluted, and the acanthus orders.

It is perhaps incorrect to say that there is no new element in Roman ornament. I believe the shell, which in after times became so very prominent, is first found in the modillion of the arch of Titus at Rome. The arch, too, is a Roman feature: where the Greeks were in the habit of using the horizontal entablature, the Romans very often have employed the arch. The Roman acanthus likewise has a character of its own. The Greeks used the Acanthus spinosus, or narrow prickly acanthus; the Romans the Acanthus mollis, or soft acanthus,—the brank-ursine of our islands. But the Roman acanthus, for capitals, is commonly composed of conventional clusters of olive-leaves; a modification arising out of the necessity for strong effect in the massive lofty temples of the Romans: but this peculiar conventional leaf does not occur otherwise than on the capitals.

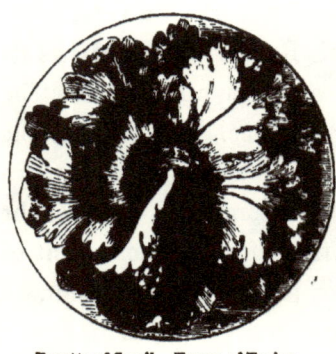

Rosette of Scroll. Forum of Trajan.

There is, further, this distinction between the two styles, that the most rarely used elements among the Greeks are the most characteristic of the Roman decorations; namely, the scroll and the acanthus;—indeed, every form which will admit of it is habitually enriched with an acanthus clothing or foliations. The acanthus, in every form except in the capitals, is so peculiarly Roman, that its appearance in an ornamental work is good presumptive evidence of its belonging to the Roman period,— or at earliest about a century subsequent to Alexander. The difference of the two leaves used, however, will effectually prevent misconception on this point. The same may be said of the scroll, in anything like an elaborate development: it is peculiarly Roman, and it is seldom without the acanthus foliations. Roman buildings are uniformly more massive than Greek, as well as bolder in their details: their curves are much fuller, — the Romans using the circular, where the Greeks generally used the elliptical. Some Roman examples of the echinus, from this fulness of curve, are especially bold and magnificent in effect. They are occasionally also remarkable for their deep under-cutting.

Acanthus Scroll, Rome.

Frieze, Forum of Trajan.

The free introduction of monsters and animals is likewise a characteristic of Greek and Roman ornament,—as the sphynx, the triton, the griffin, and others : they occur, however, much more abundantly in the Roman. The most splendid Roman ornamental specimens are those which have been dug up among the ruins of the Forum of Trajan, of the early part of the second century of our era. They are the work of a Greek,—Apollodorus of Damascus,— who carried out many great works for the Emperor Trajan.

Chimera.

CHAPTER IX.

WE have hitherto looked at only the bright side of this period: we must not overlook those features which more especially constitute it a period of decline. In the first place, quantity generally supplanted quality; and in the second, this quantity was applied in most cases without taste or propriety. This is illustrated by most of the great works of the period; and by none better than the triumphal arches, which are exclusively ornamental works.

A few remarks will suffice to show how the Roman, with its abundance of materials, was still a period of decline. It was the *use* that was made of these materials. Style and system may be looked upon as synonymous terms in ornamental art. Besides the ornaments themselves, we must have some system of applying them. And if the prominent and characteristic members of certain established styles are promiscuously thrown together, the principal features of one style applied as secondary to subordinate features of another, the value of all is diminished, and the general effect has but its vagueness to characterise it.

The same ornamental types may be used in the development of new styles,—distinction of style depending not so much on the types themselves, as on the mode of using them.

But in the development of any particular historic style of ornament, we are strictly limited to the elements belonging to that style; and in combining styles, the various members belonging to the same style should preserve their relative degree of importance.

The general decorations of the Roman period, and especially those of Pompeii, exhibit an utter disregard of these observances; and thus all distinctions of style, and consequent peculiarities of character, are lost.

The tastes of the three ancient styles,—Egyptian, Greek, and Roman,—are very distinct. The Egyptian is symbolic, rich, and severe, at the same time; the Greek is severe and beautiful; and the Roman, rich and beautiful,—at least in its good examples.

Greek taste steadily progressed until about the time of Alexander: from this period, richness and abundance of ornament gradually supplanted the chaster principles of design. The conquest of Asia introduced a taste for ornamental display, which, ending in pure ostentation, resulted in the utter annihilation of taste, and of art itself, under the luxurious example of the Roman Emperors. The Greeks themselves, however, were always lovers of splendour. Their painted and chryselephantine (gold and ivory) sculpture could hardly be surpassed in magnificence: their personal costume, as Sybaris evinces, was of the richest character; and the splendour of their temples was only characteristic of their mural decoration generally.

This splendour was carried out by the Romans on a still greater scale, until a boundless luxury established an indiscriminate extravagance of ornamental detail. Marcus Ludius, in the time of Augustus, became very celebrated

K

for his landscape decorations, which were illustrated with
figures actively employed in occupations suited to the
scenes; which kind of painting became universal after his
time, and in the first century of our era was established
that extraordinary style which we have still preserved at
Pompeii, but which the Roman writers themselves were
as far from approving as the best critics of modern times.
Vitruvius, at a still earlier time, deplores the folly and
absurdity of the stucco-work of his day. " What the
ancients," he complains, " accomplished by art, we attempt
to effect by gaudy colouring. Expense is now substituted
for skill. Who, in former times, used vermilion, except
for physic? We now cover our walls with it." Pliny
also complains of ostentation having completely supplanted
good taste in the decorations of his time: " A man now
cares nothing for art, provided he has his walls well
covered with purple, or dragon's blood from India." Vitruvius enumerates the various kinds of wall-painting in
use among the ancients. They first imitated coloured
marbles; these they afterwards divided into panels, and
enriched with ornamental frames and cornices; then architectural decorations were added; and finally were introduced tragic, comic, and satyric scenes, and landscapes.
All eventually degenerated into the existing Pompeiian
extravagances.

Yet, notwithstanding the general extravagance of this
age, there were doubtless in Rome many examples of
beautiful decoration of a very high character. Even Pompeii, an unimportant provincial town, exhibits occasional
traces of a magnificent system of decoration. The painted
figures which we find in the centres of walls or panels,

strongly relieved by their dark or coloured grounds, are
sometimes extremely beautiful in their conception, though
of inferior execution ; and some examples of scrolls and
arabesques (the most characteristic form of these decorations) likewise upon dark grounds, are, in a few instances,

Ruins at Baalbec.

of a gorgeous character of colour, and chaste in their
curves. And the mosaic and tesselated pavements discovered in Pompeii, however inappropriate in their application to floors, are examples of an exuberance of ornament
to which few, if any, modern palaces can offer a parallel ;
as, for instance, the great mosaic, measuring about twenty

feet by ten, representing the battle between Darius and Alexander at Issus, discovered in the so-called House del Fauno, in 1831. It is one of the most important relics of ancient art, and shows that though the laws of perspective are generally grossly disregarded in the architectural decorations, it was not from the ignorance of their existence; for in this work, however careless the mechanical execution may be, perspective is appreciated, and the foreshortening of the figure and the horse is even skilfully expressed. It is a work, in composition, general attitude of the figures and horses, and for treatment of costume, in every way worthy of a great master; and the picture or composition itself evidently belongs to a period long anterior to the execution of the mosaic, in which we most probably have an example of the higher school of painting of the Greeks, and possibly a coarse copy of the great battle-piece of the victory of Alexander over Darius, mentioned by Pliny, by which Philoxenus of Eretria had rendered his name celebrated.

MEDIEVAL STYLES.

FOUR LECTURES.*

CHAPTER X.

BYZANTINE ORNAMENT.

ILLUSTRATED LITERATURE.

COTMAN AND TURNER.—Architectural Antiquities of Normandy, by J. S. Cotman; accompanied by historical and descriptive notices by Dawson Turner. 2 vols. folio. London, 1822.

MUNTER, F.—Early Christian Symbolism. Sinnbilder und Kunstvorstellungen der alten Christen. 4to. Altona, 1825.

BUNSEN, C. C. J.—The Basilicas of Christian Rome, in illustration of the Idea and History of Church Architecture.

Die Basiliken des Christlichen Roms nach ihrem zusammenhange mit Idee und Geschichte der Kirchenbaukunst. 4to. Munich, 1848. (To serve as Text to the Illustrated Work of Gutensohn and Knapp. Folio. Munich, 1822-27.)

HEIDELOFF, C.—Collection of Architectural Ornaments of the Middle Ages in the Byzantine and Gothic Styles. 4 vols. 4to. Nuremberg.

---

* MEDIEVAL ART, 1849.

Syllabus.

LECTURE I.—ON EARLY CHRISTIAN AND BYZANTINE ART.

The so-called Dark Ages, from the Fourth to the Thirteenth Century. General Decay of Ancient Art. The Destructions. Constantinople or Byzantium. Establishment of Christianity. Symbolism. Prohibition of Images—Early Symbols—the Monogram—the Fish ($i\chi\theta\acute{v}\varsigma$)—*Vesica Piscis*. The Lily. The Catacombs. Images of Christ. The Nimbus or Glory. Trefoil—Quatrefoil, &c. Ancient Basilicas. Tribune. Apsis. Mosaics. Modes of Benediction—Distinction between Greek and Latin form. Monasteries of Mount Athos. The Image Controversy between the Pope and the Emperor of the East. The Iconoclasts. Sanction of Images by the Council of Nice, A.D. 787.

Ornamental Types—Cross—Dome—Circle. St. Sophia of Constantinople, A.D. 562. San Vitale, Ravenna; St. Mark's, Venice. Symbolism pervading all Designs—Examples—The Byzantine Leaf—Runic Tracery—Embroidery. Illumination of MSS. Religious Cycles.

KNIGHT, H. GALLY.—The Normans in Sicily, being a Sequel to "An Architectural Tour in Normandy." 8vo. London, 1838.

———— The Ecclesiastical Architecture of Italy, from the Time of Constantine to the fifteenth Century; with an Introduction and Text. 2 vols. folio. London, 1842-44.

———— Saracenic and Norman Remains, to illustrate "The Normans in Sicily." Folio. London, *n. d.*

MESSINA.—Roof of the Cathedral of Messina.

Charpente de la Cathédrale de Messine, dessinée par M. Morey, gravée et lithographiée par H. Roux, aîné. Chromo-lithographic plates. Folio. Paris, 1841.

QUAST, A. F. VON.—Old Christian Buildings of Ravenna.

Die Alt-christlichen Bauwerke von Ravenna, vom fünften bis zum neunten Jahrhundert, Historisch geordnet und durch Abbildungen erläutert von Al. F. Von Quast. Small Folio. Berlin, 1842.

DIDRON, M.—Iconographie Chrétienne. Hist. de Dieu. 4to. Paris, 1843.

———— Handbook of Christian Iconography.

Manuel d'Iconographie Chrétienne, Grecque et Latine, avec une Introduction et des Notes. Traduit du MS. Byzantin, "Le Guide de la Peinture," par le Dr. Paul Durand. Royal 8vo. Paris, 1845.

OSTEN, F.—Les Monuments de la Lombardie depuis le VIIᵉ Siècle jusqu'au XIVᵉ. Folio. Darmstadt and Paris, 1847, *et seq.*

LECTURE II.—ON ROMANESQUE AND SARACENIC ART.

The Romanesque. Wide-spread Influence of Byzantine Ornament. Damascus. Oriental Manufactures. Saracenic Costume. Luxury of the Caliphs of Bagdad. Tributes.

Egypt—Direct Byzantine Influence—The Mosques of Cairo—of Amrou, A.D. 641—of Touloun, A.D. 876—and El Azar (the Brilliant), A.D. 981. The Pointed Arch. Saracenic Ornaments nearly identical with Byzantine. Polychromic Decorations.

Sicily—Palermo—La Ziza, the Zigzag, 1050—Byzantine Mosaics and Glass Tesselations.

Spain—Palace of Abdu-r-rhamân III., near Cordova. The Alhambra (the Red Castle), its decorations—tracery—diapers—inscriptions. General Character of Saracenic Ornament. Tapestries.

LECTURE III.—ON THE SICULO-NORMAN AND THE EARLY POINTED STYLE.

Palermo—the Cappella Palatina, the Martorana. Greek, Saracenic, and Latin Elements. Revival of Symbolism—Cefalu, 1132. Monreale. Messina, Byzantine Mosaics, and Glass Tesselations. The Pointed Arch introduced into Sicily by the Saracens in the ninth century—into England by the Normans in the twelfth.

The Saxon or early Norman Romanesque—the Round Norman or Zigzag style—the Pointed Norman, or Transition (Plantagenet). Variety of Norman Ornaments—the Zigzag, the Billet, the Tooth, &c.

WYATT, M. D.—Specimens of the Geometrical Mosaic of the Middle Ages ; with a brief Historical Notice of the Art, founded on Papers read before the Royal Institute of British Architects, the Royal Society of Arts, and the Archæological Institute of Great Britain and Ireland. Small folio. London, 1848.

CHALMERS OF AULDBAR.—The ancient sculptured Monuments of the County of Angus, including those at Meigle in Perthshire, and one at Fordoun in the Mearns. With an additional plate and explanatory text. (Privately printed and presented to the Bannatyne Club.) Large folio. Edinburgh, 1848.

PERRET, L.—The Catacombs of Rome. Catacombes de Rome; Architecture, Peintures Murales, Inscriptions, Figures, et Symboles des Pierres sépulcrales, Verres gravés sur fond d'or, Lampes, Vases, Anneaux, Instruments, &c., des Cimetières des premiers Chrétiens. 5 vols. folio. Paris, 1852, *et seq.*

(Published by the French Government, under the direction of a Commission of the Institute of France.)

CAUMONT, DE.—Archæological A B C Book.

Abécédaire, ou Rudiment d'Archéologie. Ouvrage approuvé par l'Institut des Provinces de France. (Ornamental styles, civil and military architecture, &c.) 2 vols. 8vo. Paris, 1851-53.

INKERSLEY, T.—An Inquiry into the Chronological Succession of the Styles of Romanesque and Pointed Architecture in France ; with Notices of some of the principal Buildings on which it is founded. 8vo. London, 1850.

Stained Glass—Methods of Glass Painting—Mosaic—Mosaic-stain— and the Pure and Mixed Enamel—Mosaic Enamel.
Mosaic method described by Theophilus, twelfth and thirteenth centuries. Design, hatched and smeared on Pot Metal, in Enamel Brown—the Grozing Iron. Ornaments, chiefly from the Manuscripts—of a Byzantine or Norman character—Tan-coloured Flesh—Simple and Medallion Windows—Foliage and Quarry Patterns, plain and reticulated.

LECTURE IV.—ON GOTHIC ORNAMENT—DECORATED POINTED.

The Verticality of Gothic as contrasted with the horizontal Romanesque. The Five Arches of English Architecture—the Round, the Pointed, the Ogee, the Four-centred, and the Flat.
Seven Styles of English Ecclesiastical Architecture, from Edward the Confessor (1066) to Edward VI., about five centuries—the Saxon (early Norman Romanesque)—Round Norman (Zigzag)—Pointed Norman (Transition)—Early English Gothic (introduction of the Mullion and Tracery)—Decorated—Perpendicular (Lancastrian)—and Tudor. Average duration of each style about seventy years. Characteristics. Geometrical character of Gothic Art. Snow Crystals. Tracery—Soffit and Chamfer Cusping. The Trefoil Leaf—the Crocket—the Finial—the Gargoyle. The Tudor Flower. Manufactures.

Ruskin, J.—The Stones of Venice. 3 vols. 8vo. London, 1851.

——— Examples of the Architecture of Venice, selected and drawn to measurement from the edifices. Folio. London, 1851.

Verneilh, F. De.—L'Architecture Byzantine en France. (St.-Front de Périgueux, et les Eglises à coupoles de l'Aquitaine.) 4to. Paris, 1852.

Runge, L.—Contributions towards the Knowledge of the Brick Architecture of Italy.

Beiträge zur Kentniss der Backstein Architectur Italiens. 2 vols. folio. Berlin, 1852-53.

Blavignac, J. D.—Histoire de l'Architecture sacrée du quatrième au dixième Siècle, dans les anciens évêchés de Genève, Lausanne, et Sion. 8vo. text; atlas, ob. folio. Paris, 1853.

Quast, F. Von.—The Romanesque Cathedrals of the Middle Rhine, at Mayence, Speier, and Worms, critically and historically examine d.

Die Romanischen Dome des Mittelrheins zu Mainz, Speier, Worms. Kritisch untersucht und historisch festgestellt, durch F. Von Quast. 8vo. plates. Berlin, 1853.

Kreutz, G. et L.—La Basilica di San Marco, in Venezia, esposta ne' suoi Mosaici, e nelle sue Sculture, con illustrazione. Folio. Venice, 1843.

——— The Secondary Mosaics of the Basilica of St. Mark, Venice.

Mosaici Secondarii non compresi negli speccati geometrici, ma che completano con essi tutto l'Interno della Basilica di San Marco. 4to. Venice, 1854.

Salzenberg, W.—Old Christian Architectural Monuments of Constantinople, from the Fifth to the Twelfth Century. St. Sophia.

Alt-Christliche Baudenkmale von Constantinopel vom V. bis XII. jahrhundert. Auf befehl seiner majestät des Königs aufgenommen und historisch erläutert von W. Salzenberg. Im anhange des Silentiarius Paulus beschreibung der Heiligen Sophia und des Ambon. Metrisch übersetzt und mit anmerkungen versehen von Dr. C. W. Kortüm. Herausgegeben von dem Königl. Ministerium für Handel Gewerbe und öffentliche arbeiten. Folio. Berlin, 1854.

(Published by the Prussian Government, Ministry for Commerce, Trade, and Public Works.)

Nesfield, W. E.—Specimens of Medieval Architecture, from sketches made in France and Italy. 4to. London, 1860.

Stained Glass—Mosaic-stain—fourteenth and fifteenth centuries—Pot Metal, Stained and Coated Glass—Abrasion. Ornaments—Simple and Medallion Windows—Canopied Figures—White Flesh—Yellow Hair. Quarry, Diaper, Flower, Damask, and White or *Grisailles* patterns, in Enamel Brown.

Enamel and Mosaic Enamel, or Pure and Mixed Enamel, from the sixteenth century—Ordinary Enamel Colours on White and Coloured Glass (Pot Metal). Canopied Figures, Historic and Heraldic Designs —Floral, Geometric, Renaissance, and Cinquecento Ornament.

Bock, F.—Les Trésors sacrés de Cologne. Objets d'Art du Moyen Age. 8vo. Paris, 1860.

Tymms and Wyatt.—The Art of Illuminating, as practised in Europe from the earliest times. Illustrated by borders, initial letters, and alphabets, selected and chromolithographed by W. R. Tymms. With an Essay and Instructions by M. Digby Wyatt. Imp. 8vo. London, 1860.

WE may now turn to the Middle-Age styles, which, in contradistinction to the ancient,—the *heathen*,—may be termed *Christian* art.

The peculiar views of the early Christians in matters of art had, before the establishment of Christianity by the State, no material influence upon society, though the Pagan idolatries found many bold and vigorous opponents long before the time of Constantine. During the first and second centuries, Christian works of art were limited to symbols, and were then never applied as decorations, but as exhortations to faith and piety. And all Christian decoration rests upon this foundation,—the same spirit of symbolism prevailing throughout, until the return to the heathen principle of beauty (to the æsthetic) in the period of the Renaissance.

The early symbols were the monogram of Christ: the lily; the cross; the serpent; the fish; the aureole, or *Vesica piscis*, representing the acrostic symbol, the fish, from the common Greek word for fish, ἰχθύς, containing the initials of the following sentence: Ἰησοῦς Χριστὸς Θεοῦ Υἱός Σωτηρ,—Jesus Christ, of God the Son, the Saviour; and the circle, or *nimbus*, the glory of the head, as the *Vesica* is of the entire body. These are very important elements in Christian decoration,—especially the nimbus, which is the element of the trefoil and quatrefoil, so common in

Byzantine and Gothic art,—the first having reference to the Trinity, the second to the four Evangelists, as the testimony of Christ, and to the cross; at the extremities of which we often find four circles, besides the circle in the centre, which signifies the Lord.

Thus, figures or combinations of three, four, and five circles are common in medieval art, and have all sacred significations. Many crosses are composed nearly exclusively of the five circles as principals, or are prominently decorated with them. A cross of this character is not uncommon, either with the circle or *nimbus* in the centre, and four other circles or *nimbi* at the extremities, or composed simply of five circles arranged in the form of the cross,—the centre circle, or *nimbus*, having reference to the Lord, and the other four to the Evangelists. Occasionally the symbolic images of the Evangelists, — the angel, the lion, the ox, and the eagle,—are represented within these circles.

From a Gold Fibula.

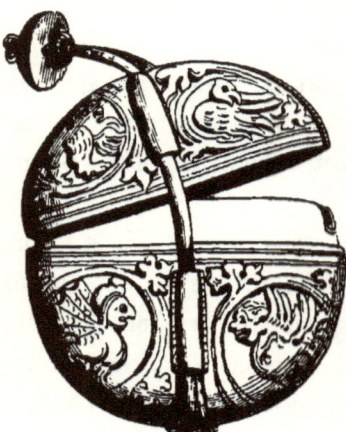

Old Leather Case.

These symbolic images of the Evangelists are frequently

applied as the principal decoration of a façade, and are constantly met with under the arches of doorways, on either side of the *vesica*, which is found circumscribing the image of Christ, with his right hand raised in the attitude of benediction.

The hand, in the attitude of benediction, is another characteristic element in early Christian and medieval works of art. There is a distinction between the Greek and the Latin form,—the Greek symbolising Jesus Christ, expressing his Greek monogram, IC.XC., (JesouC XristoC), by placing the thumb on the third finger, and slightly curving the second and fourth : the Latin displaying the thumb and the first and second fingers only extended, and thus symbolising the Trinity. The Roman prelate blesses in the name of the Trinity ; the Greek in the name of Jesus Christ.

Without some knowledge of these essential points, the Byzantine decorations are quite unintelligible ; for their early designers would appear to have avoided rather than sought beauty in all these peculiar forms : the principle is exactly the same as that by which  Egyptian art was regulated. The Lily, too (the fleur-de-lis), the emblem of the Virgin and of purity, is as common in Christian decoration as the lotus is in that of Egypt. It is the symbol which was eventually elaborated into the most characteristic foliage of Byzantine and Romanesque art, still well illustrated in work of the twelfth and thirteenth centuries,—and especially in the old iron-work of that time.

Conspicuous in their foliage, also, is a peculiarly formal and sharp version, if I may so call it, of the Greek acanthus-leaf, somewhat resembling the ordinary thistle, or holly-leaf.

Why the beautiful and accomplished styles of the ancients, then, were discarded for such comparatively crude elements of ornament, needs no other explanation than the simple statement that they were Pagan.

Architrave, St. Denis.

Paganism, however, consisted solely in forms, not in colours, and therefore, in respect of colour, there never was any restriction in Byzantine art. The forms of the ancients, too, as Paganism itself gradually disappeared, were slowly admitted among the elements of Christian decoration; and the scroll, under certain symbolic modifications,—the foliations terminating in lilies or leaves of three, four, and five blades, the number of the blades being significant,—became eventually a very prominent feature in Byzantine decoration; and under the same modifications the anthemion, and every other ancient ornament, was gradually adopted, after a systematic exclusion of about four or five centuries. But the most characteristic of all the ordinary Byzantine ornamental details, is that conventional foliage and scroll work just described.

The very exclusive prejudices of the early Byzantines once overcome, a most comprehensive style of decoration was rapidly developed, notwithstanding they never attained that purity of detail which characterises the works of the Greeks. Still, so great was their ingenuity, that they made, from their crudest symbols even, very beautiful and attractive designs.

An important feature always to be observed in the works of the Byzantines is, that all their imitations of natural forms were invariably conventional: so far they have preserved the ancient custom throughout. It is the same even with animals and with the human figure: every saint had his prescribed colours, proportions, and symbols.

This Byzantine system of decoration was fully matured, and is still shown in perfection in the rich mosaics of St. Sophia at Constantinople, completed by the Emperor Justinian 562 A.D.*

The beauty and effect of Byzantine designs is, however, as often owing to their materials as to the fashion of the ornaments themselves; and this is the case with nearly all early middle-age art; as it was with the Egyptians, and must perhaps always be in every style which depends for its individuality of character chiefly upon its symbolism: for symbols are not chosen for their *beauty*, but for their *meaning*.

---

* Some beautiful specimens have been lately published in the work of Salzenberg, on Constantinople, undertaken under the auspices of the Prussian Government.

We shall find that the most beautiful Byzantine designs are those in which the symbolism is unobtrusive, or even wholly disguised: not absent, for that is very rarely, if ever, the case. A design which contained no trace of symbolism could hardly be a genuine Byzantine example. Generally speaking, but especially in ecclesiastical decoration,—whether metal-work, stone-work, wood-carving, glass-staining, or mosaic, the symbols, in some form or other, are paramount, being mixed only

with geometrical forms. Many Byzantine capitals may appear to contradict this; but on examination it will be found that the apparently floral forms are combinations only of the conventional types derived from the symbols; as vesicas, circles, lilies, and many others. The very tracery is sometimes composed of serpents; and serpents are not an uncommon ornament for a capital.

The serpent figures largely in Byzantine art, as the instrument of the Fall, and one type of the Redemption. The cross planted on the serpent is found sculptured on Mount Athos; and the cross, surrounded by the so-called Runic knot, is only a Scandinavian version of the original Byzantine image,—the crushed snake curling round the stem of the avenging cross. The cross, with two scrolls at the foot of it, typifying the snake, is another of its modifications, and a very common Byzantine ornament. The ordinary northern crosses, so conspicuous for their interlaced ornaments and grotesque monsters, appear to be purely modifications of this idea. Some good examples

Iron Hinge, Notre-Dame, Paris.

may be seen in Chalmers' *Sculptured Monuments of Angus.*

The leading forms of Byzantine architecture are likewise due to the same influence—the cross, the circle, and the dome, pervade everywhere. The dome has its own reference to the vault of heaven, whose living glories were generally represented on the spherical roof of the apse at the end of the Greek Basilicas. This representation is known in the Greek Church as the holy liturgy, or the glorification of Christ, and it often illustrates the dome itself in the centre of the cross. This is the reason that the cross and the dome are so characteristic of early Christian or Byzantine architecture, and indeed of Romanesque architecture generally.

Some of the principal Byzantine or Romanesque churches are developments of the symbol of the five circles or glories : they are placed in the form of a cross, and are surmounted by domes corresponding in size and situation to the circles represented in the pavement below. St. Mark's at Venice is a conspicuous example of this symbolic architecture.

This species of architecture, with the dome and round arch, is termed Romanesque, as derived immediately from that which prevailed throughout the Roman Empire at that time when from heathen it became Christian : some of its classical types are the Pantheon, the Colosseum, and the palace of Diocletian at Spalatro. Though not Roman absolutely, it is derived from the Roman ; it is debased Roman—*Romanesque :* it is a general term which distinguishes the round-arch species from the Saracenic and Gothic, which are pointed-arch species. The preservation of the dome and arch, however, was probably due rather to the symbolic value of those figures among the Byzantine Greeks than to the mere historic example of the Romans.

The chief varieties of the Romanesque are — the Byzantine, the Lombard, and the Norman.* Both the Lombard and the Norman may, in a technical point of view, be considered mere modifications or varieties of the Byzantine; certainly few examples of the Romanesque out of Italy were not derived, directly or indirectly, from Constantinople, or Byzantium, as it was previously called. The style extended to this country as far north as York and Hexham : it is still the standard type in Russia; and it is the exclusive model of the whole system of architecture of the Mohammedans, from Benares to Cadiz, from Cairo to Damascus.   Indeed the Byzantine was so widely spread, and so thoroughly identified with all middle-age art, that its influence did not entirely cease until the establishment of the Renaissance in the fifteenth century : both the Saracenic and the Gothic proceeded from the Byzantine.

The Greek missionaries carried its influence into the extreme north ; and while the artists of Syria were accommodating their style to Mohammedan exclusiveness in the south, in the colder regions of Europe the mysteries of Mount Athos were freely mixed up with the fables of Scandinavian mythology.

The Scandinavian soldiers, also, of the imperial body-guard, made the talismans of Christian mythology almost

---

* See these styles beautifully illustrated in Osten's "Buildings of Lombardy."

Capital. Moissac, France.

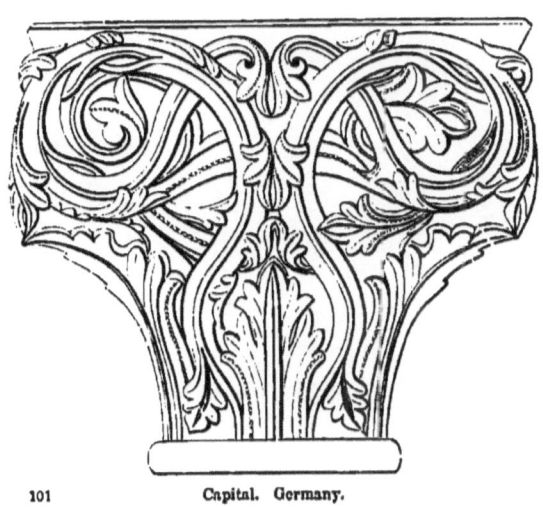

Capital. Germany.

St. Cross, Winchester.

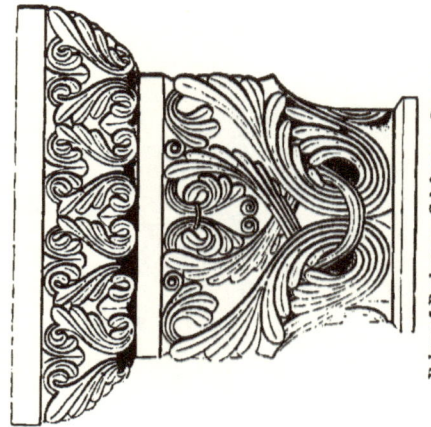

Palace of Barbarossa, Gelnhausen, Germany.

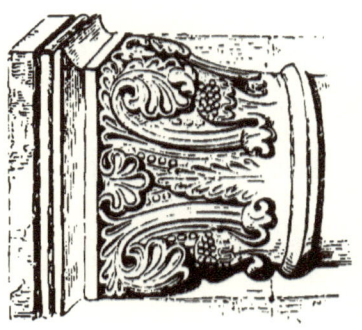

St. Cross, Winchester.

104

as familiar in their native homes as the gods of their forefathers. The same mixture became as common eventually on the portals of Lombardy.

There is this difference between the Byzantine and the Lombard and Norman varieties, that the symbolism is mere matter of habit in the two latter, and generally, perhaps, though rudely preserved in many forms, is disregarded in their spirit; that is, in mere ornamental details, such as the zigzag, dog's-tooth, nail-head, star, chain, and a host of others: but the symbolic figures and other religious decorations mean exactly what they express.

As the peculiarly Norman style, such as it is best known in this country, was originally developed in Sicily, it contains, of course, many Saracenic features, of which the pointed arch and the zigzag are the most prominent; for the Norman, though originally a simple Romanesque style, eventually adopted in the twelfth century the pointed arch of the Mohammedans.* This style is well developed in the Cathedral of Cefalu in Sicily, built by King Roger in 1132.

The terms Byzantine and Romanesque have been used above as almost synonymous. They are so as regards their architectural features; the Byzantine being only a variety of the Romanesque. In the later centuries they may be considered the same in all respects; but in the earlier centuries there is an ornamental distinction: the more strictly Romanesque, or Latin, being a simple debasement of Roman art; the Byzantine, or Greek, being this art combined with the symbolic elements

---

* Gally Knight, "Saracenic and Norman Remains in Sicily."

M

introduced by the new Christian religion, comprising a peculiar symbolic version also of the old Roman acanthus foliage. The wider signification of the *Romanesque*, however, is the earlier Christian round arch developments, in contradistinction to the Gothic, or later pointed arch varieties of the North. If any style can be distinguished with the exclusive title of *Christian Architecture*, it is the Byzantine, of which St. Sophia, at Constantinople, is a magnificent type.

Byzantine Frieze, from a Church at Bonn.

CHAPTER XI.

SARACENIC ORNAMENT.

ILLUSTRATED LITERATURE.

MURPHY, J. C.—The Arabian Antiquities of Spain; representing in 100 engravings the Principal Remains of the Architecture, Sculpture, Paintings, and Mosaics of the Spanish Arabs, from Drawings made on the spot. Large folio. London, 1816.

COSTE, P.—Architecture Arabe, ou Monumens du Kaire, mesurés et dessinés de 1817 à 1826. Folio. Paris, 1837—39.

KNIGHT, H. GALLY.—The Normans in Sicily; being a sequel to "An Architectural Tour in Normandy." 8vo. London, 1838.

———— Saracenic and Norman Remains, to illustrate "The Normans in Sicily." Folio. London, n. d.

DE PRANGEY, G.—Essai sur l'Architecture des Arabes et des Mores en Espagne, en Sicile, et en Barbarie. Royal 8vo. Paris, 1841.

JONES AND GOURY.—Plans, Elevations, Sections, and Details of the Alhambra. From Drawings taken on the spot in 1834 by the late M. Jules Goury, and in 1834 and 1837 by Owen Jones. With a complete Translation of the Arabic Inscriptions, and an Historical Notice of the Kings of Granada from the Conquest of that city by the Arabs to the Expulsion of the Moors, by M. Pasqual de Gayangos. Folio. London, 1842.

HESSEMER.—Saracenic and Old Italian Building Decorations. Arabische und Alt-Italienische Bau-verzierungen. 120 chromolithographs. 2nd edition, folio. Berlin, 1853.

BISSON, M.—Choix d'Ornements Arabes de l'Alhambra, offrant dans leur ensemble une synthèse de l'ornementation Mauresque en Espagne au XIIIᵉ Siècle. Reproduits en photographe. 4to. Paris, 1853.

Cairo.

WE will now consider the second medieval style—the
Saracenic. Its principles are soon stated : the Arabs had
not art or artists of their own ; they came from their
deserts, with no more taste or knowledge of such matters
than a mere love of finery could give them ; they could
not but be struck by the gorgeous display of such cities
as Damascus, which fell into their hands in 634 A.D. ;
new ambitions arose with their new power, and the
Byzantine artists were pressed into the service of the
Arabian caliphs and generals, and ordered to raise rich
mosques and palaces. Damascus, Cairo, and Cordova,
show the admirable ingenuity with which they accommo-
dated themselves to their new circumstances. The conditions of the new Mohammedan law were stringent : in
endless designs in mosaic, marquetry, or in stucco, there
was to be no image of a living thing, vegetable or animal.
Such conditions led to a very individual style of decoration : vegetable forms were now excluded for the first

time. However, by the seventh century, when the works of the Saracens commenced, the Byzantine Greeks were already sufficiently skilful to make light of such exclusions, and the exertion of ingenuity which they impelled gave rise to a more beautiful simply ornamental style than perhaps any that had preceded it, for there was no division of the artistic mind now between meaning and effect; and although the religious cycles and other symbolic figures which had hitherto engrossed so much of the artist's attention were excluded, the mere conventional ornamental symbolism, the ordinary forms borrowed from the classic periods, and geometrical symmetry, left an abundant field behind, which was further enriched by the peculiarly Saracenic custom of elaborating inscriptions into their designs. Mere curves and angles or interlacings were now to bear the chief burden of a design, but distinguished by a variety of colour; the curves, however, very naturally fell into the standard forms and floral shapes, and the lines and angles were soon developed into a very characteristic species of tracery or interlaced strap-work, very agreeably diversified by the ornamental introduction of the inscriptions. And although flowers were not palpably admitted, the great mass of the minor details of Saracenic designs are composed of flower forms disguised; the very inscriptions are sometimes thus grouped as flowers: this is especially the case in the later works of the Alhambra; still no actual flower ever occurs, as the exclusion of all natural images is the fundamental of the style in its purity.

The omission of the crescent in Saracenic or Mohammedan work generally is worth notice. It now crowns, the great mosques of Constantinople, but it is not to be found in any early work, and it appears to be itself simply the trophy of the conquest of the Greek capital of Constantinople, the ancient Byzantium, of which it was the symbol, the town on one occasion having, according to an old tradition, been preserved from a night ambuscade by the timely appearance of the new moon; it occurs on old Byzantine coins. Constantinople was not captured by the Turks until 1453.

One of the greatest works produced under these circumstances was the magnificent mosque of Touloun at Cairo, a monument of the ninth century (876 A.D.), and the recorded work of a Greek. The ornaments are in stucco, and altogether offer the most characteristic example of the combination of Byzantine and Saracenic elements. With the Saracenic tracery and inscriptions, and other peculiar forms, we have combined several of the most popular ancient ornaments in their Byzantine garb, but somewhat more than ordinarily modified, as the fret, anthemion, the guilloche, the horns of plenty, and the fleur-de-lis.

The more characteristic detail, that is, the original Saracenic elements, the disguised conventional foliage spoken of, is very beautifully elaborated in some of the accessory works of this mosque. They became standards to after ages; for the details of the diaper-tiles of the Alhambra, executed some five hundred years afterwards, are in many respects nearly identical with these details of the mosque of Touloun at Cairo.

In all these early Arabian buildings of Cairo we have the pointed arch, which appears first, I believe, in the

111   Alhambra Diaper.

great mosque of Amrou, a work of the seventh century
(641 A.D.); but the ogee, the crescent, and the scalloped
arches, are more characteristic, perhaps, of Saracenic
architecture generally, as the pointed arch has been
made familiar by a later style; but the simple round
Romanesque arch also occurs in the Moorish works of
Spain. This style became gradually richer as it advanced
westwards from Egypt to Sicily, and especially in Spain,
where the Alhambra, a work of the fourteenth century,
still remains to bear witness to its unparalleled richness of
detail.

There is not much pure Saracenic work in Sicily; the
palace of La Ziza, at Palermo, is, perhaps, the only
example : there are, however, some magnificent Siculo-
Norman remains of the twelfth century at Palermo,
Monreale, Cefalu, and Messina, in which Greek or
Saracenic artists were engaged; and the glass mosaics
in these places are among the finest specimens of their
class existing: they exhibit some exquisite examples of
tracery or interlacing.

The Saracenic was the period of gorgeous diapers, for
their habit of decorating the entire surfaces of their
apartments was peculiarly favourable to the development
of this class of design : the Alhambra displays almost
endless specimens, and all are in relief and enriched
with gold and colour, chiefly blue and red. Some give
the idea of being more endurable imitations of the rich
woollens of Cashmere, which the Arabs always made
great store of. The Genoa damasks, Arras tapestries,
and modern paper-hangings, are all imitations of these
Saracenic wall diapers. The very word "Damask" means

Damascus work. Damascus, however, was famous for such fabrics before its conquest by the Arabs. It was called Damesk, and was a place of repute even in the time of Abraham.

Damascus is still famous for its textile fabrics in a pure Saracenic taste, and it produces a great variety of patterns in silk and in cotton, the designs of which are chiefly stripes and inscriptions, good wishes or pious sentences.*

The Siculo-Norman, from which our round zigzag (Ziza), and the pointed Norman, are derived, is as much a variety of the Saracenic as of the Byzantine: it is indeed a free combination of the two styles; for the reserved mixture of the two hitherto practised had its Christian character restored to it by the Normans, through the introduction of sacred figures, and a prominence which they gave to all the most palpable Christian symbols, more especially

Berkeley Castle, Gloucestershire.

* This style has of late years found its way into our railway carriages: worsted borders, in which the initials of the company are worked as an ornamental pattern, right and left, and upside down, as in the Eastern examples, are now common. The mock inscriptions on the borders of rich robes, in early Italian pictures, are also derived from oriental models. The richest stuffs were from the East, and were decorated with Arabic inscriptions; the old painters accordingly, when from a spirit of veneration they dressed their saints in rich robes, were very particular in the elaboration of their border decorations, which necessarily implied a robe of a costly oriental fabric. There are several examples of such borders in the National Gallery.

the Cross, which never occurs in genuine Saracenic work. This renders the Siculo-Norman a very complete style, and it is displayed in great magnificence in the cathedral of Messina.

The Alhambra does not exhibit that Byzantine character in its details which we find in Sicily or in the Mosques of Cairo: all the peculiar Arabian features are preserved, but the scroll and anthemion, which are often in very rich development on the monuments of Cairo, can with difficulty be traced in the Alhambra. We discover the scroll in some of the interlacings, and there is a fan-shape which recalls the anthemion.

The artists of the Alhambra were probably exclusively Saracenic. The beauty of this palace is in its general richness of effect, in its endless combinations of columns, arches, and gorgeous surfaces; its gold and silver flowers, and its intricate tracery, which all combine to give the impression of extraordinary splendour as a whole, though no particular part commands any special admiration.

House at Damascus.

N

CHAPTER XII.

GOTHIC ORNAMENT.

ILLUSTRATED LITERATURE.

DE LABORDE, LE COMTE ALEXANDRE.—Les Monumens de la France, classés chronologiquement, et considérés sous le Rapport des Faits historiques et de l'Etude des Arts. 2 vols. folio. Paris, 1816—36.

CARTER, J.—The Ancient Architecture of England, including the Orders during the British, Roman, Saxon, and Norman Eras; and under the reigns of Henry III. and Edward III. Illustrated by 109 engravings. A new and improved edition, with Notes and copious Indexes, by John Britton. Folio. London, 1837.

———— Specimens of the Ancient Sculpture and Painting now remaining in England, from the earliest period to the reign of Henry VIII. Exhibited in 120 plates, drawn and etched by J. Carter. With Critical and Historical Illustrations by Francis Douce, Richard Gough, John Fenn, J. S. Hawkins, William Bray, and the Rev. J. Milner. A new and improved edition, arranged in topographical order, and illustrated with copious notes by Dawson Turner, Sir Samuel Rush Meyrick, John Britton, and others. Folio. London, 1838.

BRITTON, J.—The Cathedral Antiquities of England. 5 vols. 4to. London, 1836.

PUGIN, A. W.—Specimens of Gothic Architecture, selected from various Ancient Edifices in England, consisting of plans, elevations, sections, and parts at large, &c. The literary part by J. E. Willson. 3 vols. 3rd edition, corrected and revised. 4to. London, 1821—50.

POPP, J., AND BULEAU, TH.—The Three Ages of Gothic Architecture. Les Trois Ages de l'Architecture Gothique, son origine, sa théorie, démontrés et représentés par des Exemples choisis à Ratisbonne, &c. Folio. Paris, 1841.

BOISERÉE, S.—Histoire et Description de la Cathédrale de Cologne. Pour servir de texte aux Vues, Plans, Coupes, et Détails de l'Edifice. Nouvelle édition refaite et augmentée. Plates, folio; text, 4to. Munich, 1842—43.

KALLENBACH, G. G. VON.—A Tabular History of German Medieval Architecture.

Atlas zur Geschichte der Deutsch-Mittelalterlichen Baukunst, in 86 tafeln. Folio. Munich, 1847.

BRANDON, R. AND J. A.—An Analysis of Gothic Architecture, illustrated by a series of upwards of seven hundred examples of Doorways, Windows, &c., and accompanied with Remarks on the several details of an Ecclesiastical Edifice. 2 vols. 4to. London, 1847.

BLACKBURNE, E. L.—Sketches, Graphic and Descriptive, for a History of the Decorative Painting applied to English Architecture during the Middle Ages. 4to. London, 1847.

COLLING, J. K.—Gothic Ornaments, being a series of examples of enriched Details and Accessories of the Architecture of Great Britain. Drawn from existing authorities. 2 vols. 4to. London, 1850.

LACROIX AND SERÉ.—The Middle Ages and the Renaissance, Manners and Customs, Sciences, and Art, &c., with fac-simile illustrations.

Le Moyen Age et la Renaissance, Histoire et Description des Mœurs et Usages, du Commerce et de l'Industrie, des Sciences, des Arts, des Littératures et des Beaux Arts en Europe. Direction littéraire de M. Paul Lacroix. Direction artistique de M. Ferdinand Seré. Dessins fac-similes par M. A. Rivaud. 5 vols. 4to. Paris, 1848—51.

GAILHABAUD, J.—On Architecture from the fifth to the sixteenth century, and the Arts depending on it—Sculpture, Wall-Painting, Glass-Painting, Mosaic, Ironwork, &c.

L'Architecture du Ve au XVIe Siècle, et les Arts qui en dépendent, la Sculpture, la Peinture murale, la Peinture sur Verre, la Mosaïque, la Ferronnerie, &c., publiés d'après les travaux inédits des principaux Architectes Français et Etrangers. 4to. Paris, 1851, et seq.

BECKER AND HEFNER.—Works of Art and Utensils of the Middle Ages and the Renaissance.

Kunstwerke und Geräthschaften des Mittelalters und der Renaissance. By C. Becker and J. von Hefner. 2 vols. 4to. Frankfurt, 1852.

STROOBANT, F.—Monumens d'Architecture et de Sculpture en Belgique. Texte par Félix Stappaerts. 4to. Bruxelles, 1852.

KING, T. H.—Jewellery and Metal Work of the Middle Ages.

Orfèvrerie et Ouvrages en Métal du Moyen Age. (Designed from old examples.) Folio. Bruges, 1852, et seq.

WARING, J. B.—Architectural, Sculptural, and Picturesque Studies in Burgos and its Neighbourhood. Folio. London, 1852.

WICKES, C.—Illustrations of the Spires and Towers of the Medieval Churches of England. Preceded by some Observations on the

Architecture of the Middle Ages, and its Spire Growth. 2 vols. folio. London, 1853—55.

Dollman and Jobbins.—An Analysis of Ancient Domestic Architecture in Great Britain. 4to. London, 1860.

The third and last great middle-age style was the Gothic. Of this I can remark only as regards its general principles, to fully explain all its subdivisions of style would occupy much space.

It grew out of the Byzantine, and flourished chiefly on the Rhine, in the north of France, and in England. Salisbury Cathedral, A.D. 1221, the first great work of the kind in this country, is a work of the French, but in style it was a genuine Norman beginning. The Gothic was developed in the thirteenth century, and was perfected in the fourteenth; its most characteristic monument, perhaps, is Cologne Cathedral, which was consecrated in the year 1322; in the fifteenth century it rapidly declined, and it became quite extinct, in this country at least, in the sixteenth; a catastrophe doubtless involved by the Reformation.

England has had seven ecclesiastical styles, extending over a space of about five hundred years only, from the death of Edward the Confessor, 1066, to the death of Queen Mary, 1558, when all ecclesiastical architecture ceased; and the Tudor was superseded by the Renaissance in the reign of Elizabeth.

The seven styles are,—

1. The Saxon, or simple round arch, Romanesque.

2. The round Norman (zigzag style).

3. The pointed Norman, or transition (Henry II., or first Plantagenet style).

119   The Lynn Cup.   c. 1400.

4. The early English Gothic (Henry III., or second Plantagenet style).

5. The decorated Gothic (the Edwards, the third Plantagenet style).

6. The perpendicular Gothic (Henry VII., or Lancastrian).

7. The debased Perpendicular, or flat (Henry VIII., or Tudor).

Thus during the period of the seven Edwards there were seven styles, the duration of each of which was, on an average, about seventy years (1066—1556), or about the period of the personal influence of an individual by his own direct efforts, and that of his school or followers combined. The history of architecture shows a succession of changes in most countries, but in England these changes have been singularly rapid and regular.

In this period of the development of the ecclesiastical styles it is remarkable how little the notion of a style existed, and how regardless the builders, or masons, of one age were of the sentiment or aim of those of a previous age. Few subjects show such perfect want of accord as the building of our cathedrals. In every case where a great ecclesiastical work has been suspended, and renewed after intervals, those who have carried on the enterprise have done so invariably utterly regardless of the character of the work already executed; the practice of the day exclusively defined the character of the work, as if the practical education of the handicraftsman, his accidental skill, were the paramount source of the whole scheme and system of ornamental varieties; each mason working out only such forms as had occupied his time in the years of his apprentice-ship. There are not many matters on which the English people have been more deluded of late years than on the subject of the nationality and the *Christianity* of Gothic architecture. Gothic is of comparatively very late development, and endured at most in this country for about three centuries; it is by no means English in its origin, and so far from having any determinate unity in its character, it displays, as already shown, a continued succession of changes. Its religious elements are Byzantine. As regards *Christianity of style*, the most Christian architecture is literally that of the Mohammedan mosques, which owe their forms to the early Christian symbolism, as developed by the Byzantine Greeks.

Three only of the above styles, the fourth, fifth, and sixth, are what can be strictly termed Gothic: the two first are round arch, and belong to the Byzantine or Romanesque varieties; the third is the simple transition from the round to the pointed styles; and the seventh is the transition back again from those styles in which the arch is so prominent a feature, to the Renaissance varieties, in which the arch becomes again round, and loses its importance as a principal elementary feature of style.

The general characteristics of the Gothic, as an architectural style, are these:—It is essentially pointed or vertical in its tendency, and in its detail is geometrical—in its window-tracery, in its openings, in its clusters of shafts and bases, and in its suits of mouldings—but it is only geometrical in its construction, or in its form, not in its spirit or motive.

All the symbolic elements of the Byzantine are continued in the Gothic; but the pointed arch is substituted for the round. There is a close traditional connection in all the ordinary details, though the virulence of the image controversy, and other · differences, between the Greek and Latin Churches, doubtless had some influence in the development of a change of style; for we find that where the Greek Church has prevailed · there has been, until very recently, no essential change whatever in ecclesiastical architecture. It is unquestionable, how- ever, that climate has had something to do also with the peculiar development of the Gothic; it has flourished only in cold regions subject to much rain and snow, and a Gothic church frequently looks very like a fortification against the weather, with its high-pitched roof, solid buttresses, and narrow doors and windows. As I have already explained, the pointed arch, one of the charac- teristics of the Gothic, is not peculiar to it; it had already existed five hundred years in Egypt, and is the common form of the Siculo-Norman arch.

The Gothic is chiefly distinguished from the Byzantine and the Latin Romanesque varieties, by the universal absence of the dome, and the substitution of the pointed for the round arch. The union of the belfry with the church is not peculiar to the Gothic, though in the great Romanesque examples they are distinct, as at Venice and Pisa; they are also distinct at Florence, and many other Italian towns; nor are the towers in the place of the domes peculiar to the Gothic, they are common in the Norman Romanesque in Sicily, in Germany, and in this country, as at Ely, Peterborough, and elsewhere. The spire is the pointed roof of the tower, and both doubtless originally owed their development as much to use as to ornament: in thinly-populated and only half-cleared countries, such as England was in the Middle Ages, a tower or spire was a landmark performing other useful services besides that of simply indicating the locality of the church, or securing the proper elevation of its bells.

The transition added the spire to the old tower of the Romanesque and Norman, and it is a common feature of the Gothic; while the square abacus and the heavy cushion capitals of these styles, with their simple incised ornaments, are converted, in the transition, to the round abacus and the bell-shaped capital, decorated with raised foliage, and eventually elaborated into infinite variety in the Gothic styles.

Ornamentally the Gothic is the geometrical and pointed element elaborated to its utmost, its only peculiarities are its combinations of details; at first the conventional and the geometrical prevailing, and afterwards these combined with the elaboration of natural objects in its decoration. The Byzantines never did this, their ornaments were purely conventional; while in the finest Gothic specimens we find not only the traditional conventional ornaments, but in the decorated period also elaborate imitations of the plants and flowers growing in the neighbourhood of the work. This is a great feature; but still the most striking feature of all Gothic work is the wonderful elaboration of its geometric tracery—vesicas, trefoils, quatrefoils, cinquefoils, and an infinity of geometric varieties besides. The tracery is so paramount a characteristic that the three English varieties,

Spandril, Stone Church, Kent.

Crocket, Lincoln.

Tooth Ornament, Stone Church, Kent.

.M. RESS.

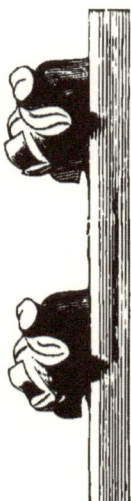

Crockets, Lincoln.

the Early English, the Decorated, and the Perpendicular, are distinguished almost exclusively by this feature; it is the same with the French flamboyant—the flame style, from the waving lines of its tracery. The tracery, indeed, establishes the fact of a style being Gothic or not, for the Byzantine contains only the symbolic foliations; so the pointed style called "Transition" is not Gothic, because it has no tracery.

The first Gothic in this country is the Early English, in which we have the first development of geometrical

From the Temple Church.

window-tracery; mullions instead of piers; windows of several lights; flying buttresses, crocketed pinnacles, complicated mouldings, the columns clustered, and the capitals generally round; an extensive application of foliage, with the trefoil leaf, commonly called the Early-English leaf, as the most characteristic ornament. It is sometimes as formal as a clover leaf, at other times very irregularly formed, but always with a fulness or roundness of the parts, as contrasted with the somewhat similar, but flat or even

o

hollow Byzantine or Norman foliage, of which it is a
variation.

The so-called tooth, or dog's-tooth, the most characteristic ornamental detail of the previous pointed style, the
Transition, occurs comparatively rarely in the Early
English, and in the early specimens only, and consider-
ably varied in detail. This ornament was probably in its
original form a simple vesica cross, but being contracted
to fill hollows was developed into its ordinary character,
so common in early Plantagenet, or Transition work.

Upon the Early English succeeded the Decorated, chiefly
characterised by a more magnificent development of the
leading elements of the Early English, more especially the
tracery; but it has its own features—the ogee arch, and
the pinnacled canopied recesses of the buttresses, and other
parts, producing a prominence of diagonal lines. The
so-called ball-flower, and the common serpentine vine-
scroll, are the most characteristic details of this period.
There is also more nature, or imitation, in the details than
in any other of the Gothic varieties.

In the third variety, the Perpendicular, the new features
are the horizontal line, the panellings, and the substitution
of perpendicular for flowing tracery. And the execution
of the ornamental details is very conventional. The most
prominent bar of the tracery is the mullion itself, so that
the prevalent panelling of the style is also prominent in
the window tracery, composed of mullion upon mullion, or
mullion and supermullion, being separated by a horizontal
bar, termed a transom. This divides the lights into vertical
panes or panels, and the same panelling (of which fan-
tracery is also an example) is spread over every surface of

Pedestal, Henry VII.'s Chapel.

the buildings of this period, developing that style which I have termed Lancastrian, commonly known as the Perpendicular: it is the great style of the fifteenth century in this country.

The natural freedom of the details occasionally displayed in the Decorated, is now lost in a formal conventionality in the Perpendicular; which displays an execution of these parts much more analogous to German work, and the original Byzantine elements from which Gothic forms generally were indirectly derived. The crockets also of perpendicular work are, like the foliage, very formal, exhibiting a square cruciform arrangement in the details of the leaves, and a uniform character, more analogous to sea-weed than ordinary leaves, in the foliage generally.

The Tudor is scarcely a Gothic; the art in it returns to what it was in the Roman-esque, and again becomes horizontal. Its great features are the flat arch, the square dripstone, and the rectangular spandril, a necessary development of the square dripstone over the arch. The running ornament known as the Tudor-flower, and conspicuous, because almost alone, in buildings of this charac-

All Saints, Fearing, Essex.

ter, is a remnant of the old Byzantine. Its name of Tudor-flower is appropriate only in the sense that it is almost the only medieval ornament preserved in that style: the original type of this ornament is the old Byzantine alternation of the lily and the cross, common as the decoration of a crown, and for edges or borders of many other kinds.

There are five orders of arches which distinguish these several ecclesiastical styles generally, namely—the round, the pointed, the ogee, the four-centred, and the flat: the pointed itself comprising three varieties—the lancet, the pointed, and the drop arch; in the first the pitch being greater than the span, in the second equal to it, and in the last less.

In ornamental art generally, then, as in architecture, it is geometrical tracery which will stamp a design with a Gothic character: decorate it with natural flowers only, it will still be Gothic; it would be necessarily made much more characteristic by the introduction of some of the historic ornaments of the period,—as the Tudor-flower, fleur-de-lis, crocket-leaf, trefoil or Early English leaf, vine-scroll, or any other of the more familiar ornaments of the style. As, however, the Gothic is a style which has flourished exclusively in cold countries, its ornaments of a natural class to be characteristic should be from such plants as are native to Gothic latitudes; tropical plants would be inconsistent. Throughout we should prefer the wild plants of the north to the more exuberant flowers of the south. All exotics, in fact, that are not symbols, should be unconditionally excluded. The characteristic Norman ornaments are not admissible in the Gothic, with the exception of the tooth, and that is peculiarly rendered.

Classical ornaments, likewise, are of course excluded; even the scroll occurs only in the Gothic as a serpentine. Gothic ornaments independent of the tracery are nearly exclusively fruit, flowers, or leaves; and as a general rule, the execution is extremely rude.

Such is a rough outline of the course of ornamental art among the most prominent people of medieval history, for a period of more than a thousand years. We have seen that all varieties, however individual in character, are intimately connected with those which preceded them; an advantage once gained was not allowed to be lost; and the remarkable transition from the Byzantine to the Saracenic, so totally different in spirit and in detail, yet both developed by the same artists, shows that it is not from a persevering manual routine that variety and beauty are to be derived, but from the active intelligence of the controlling mind.

Fountains Abbey, Yorkshire.

MODERN OR RENAISSANCE STYLES.

FOUR LECTURES.*

CHAPTER XIII.

ILLUSTRATED LITERATURE.

JUVARRA, CAV. D. F.—Collection of Shields, from the Originals in Rome. Raccolta di Targhe fatte da' Professori primari in Roma, disegnate, ed intagliate dal Cav. D. Filippo Juvarra. (Renaissance Sculpture.) 4to. Rome, 1722.

BALTARD.—Paris et ses Monumens, mesurés, dessinés, et gravés, avec des Descriptions historiques par le Citoyen Amaury Duval : Louvre, St. Cloud, Fontainebleau, Château d'Ecouen, &c. 2 vols. large folio. Paris, 1803-5.

WILLEMIN, N. X.—Monuments Francais inédits pour servir à l'Histoire des Arts, depuis le VIᵉ Siècle jusqu'au commencement du XVIIᵉ. Choix de Costumes civils et militaires, d'Armes, Armures, Instruments de Musique, Meubles de toute espèce, et de Décorations intérieures et extérieures des Maisons. Dessinés, gravés, et coloriés d'après les originaux. Classés chronologiquement et accompagnés d'un texte historique et descriptif, par André Pottier. 6 vols. small folio. Paris, 1806-39.

---

* ON THE ORNAMENT OF THE RENAISSANCE, 1849-50.
Syllabus.

LECTURE I.—INTRODUCTION—THE TRECENTO.

The Renaissance (Rinascimento), or Revival. Definition—Varieties. The Trecento (1300) dates from about the Venetian Conquest of Constantinople, 1204 A.D. Interlacings and delicate Scroll-work of Conventional Foliage. Byzantine, in its original elements ; a mixture of Venetian and Siculo-Norman Ornament.

The great Artists, the great Decorators—Maestro Lapo, Arnolfo di Lapo, Giunta Pisano, Niccola Pisano, Giotto, Orcagna, Brunelleschi, Alberti. Revival of the Round Arch and the Classical Orders.

SOMMERARD, A. DU.—Les Arts au Moyen Age. (Collection of the Hôtel de Clugny.) Text, 5 vols. 8vo.; plates, 6 vols. folio. Paris, 1836-46.

LACROIX AND SERÉ.—The Middle Ages and the Renaissance, Manners and Customs, Sciences and Arts, &c.; with fac-simile illustrations.

Le Moyen Age et la Renaissance, Histoire et Description des Mœurs et Usages du Commerce et de l'Industrie, des Sciences, des Arts, des Littératures, et des Beaux Arts en Europe. Direction littéraire de M. Paul Lacroix. Direction artistique de M. Ferdinand Seré. Dessins fac-similes par M. A. Rivaud. 5 vols. 4to. Paris, 1848-51.

BECKER AND HEFNER.—Works of Art and Utensils of the Middle Ages and the Renaissance.

Kunstwerke und Geräthschaften des Mittelalters und der Renaissance. By C. Becker and J. von Hefner. Many coloured plates, 2 vols. 4to. Frankfort, 1852.

RUSSIAN EMPIRE.—Ecclesiastical, Imperial, and other Antiquities of the Russian Empire. Published by Supreme Command. (Russian text.) Produced under the direction of an Imperial Commission. By S. Stroganov, M. Zagoskin, J. Snegirev, and A. Th. Veltman. Division 1. Ecclesiastical Antiquities; 2. Imperial Insignia, Dresses, &c.; 3. Arms and Armour; 4. Costume, Pictures, and Portraits; 5. Furniture, Jewellery, &c.; 6. Architecture and Decoration. Text, 6 vols. 4to.; plates, 6 vols. folio. St. Petersburg, 1852.

DURELLI, G. AND F.—The Charter House of Pavia.

La Certosa di Pavia descritta ed illustrata con tavole incise dai fratelli Gaetano e Francesco Durelli. 62 plates. Folio. Milan, 1853.

BERAIN, JEAN.—Collection of Ornamental Designs. Mural Chimney-pieces, and other Decorations, Cinquecento, Renaissance, and Louis

---

LECTURE II.—THE RENAISSANCE—THE QUATTROCENTO.

The Quattrocento (1400). Tradition superseded by Selection. Natural Imitations in the Details, and the symmetrical Arabesques from Ancient Sculpture, added to the elements of the previous style, with occasional Cartouches, or scrolled Shield-work. Luca della Robbia —Enamelled Pottery. Andrea Pisano. Iron and Bronze work—The Gates of the Baptistery of San Giovanni at Florence. Lorenzo Ghiberti, 1403—52. Niello-work. Tommaso Finiguerra. Metal-plate engraving, 1452. The Renaissance as an Epoch and as a Style.

LECTURE III.—THE CINQUECENTO.

The Cinquecento (1500), the predominant Italian style of the Sixteenth Century, the ultimate goal of the Renaissance. A perfect restoration of Classical Ornament of the Roman period, to the exclusion of all alien forms, with an especial elaboration of the Arabesques and Scrolls, and grotesque combinations of Vegetable and Animal Forms: a purely æsthetic, or sensuous development of Ornament.

Quatorze. 137 plates, engraved by Daigremont, Scotin, and others. Folio. Paris, c. 1670—1700.

BERAIN, CHAUVEAU, AND LE MOINE.—Decorations of the Apollo Gallery, Louvre, &c.

Ornemens de Peinture et de Sculpture, qui sont dans la Galerie d'Apollon, au Château du Louvre, et dans le grand Appartement du Roy au Palais des Tuileries. Dessinez et gravez par les Sieurs Berain, Chauveau, et Le Moine. (Fine examples of the Renaissance and the Louis Quatorze.) Folio. Paris, 1710.

LEPAUTRE.—Collection des plus belles Compositions de Lepautre. Folio. Paris, 1854.

VERSAILLES.—Souvenir d'une Promenade à Versailles. Vues Inté-rieures. Folio. Paris, 1843.

PALMER, C. F.—The History and Illustrations of a House in the Eliza-bethan Style of Architecture, the property of John Danby Palmer, Esq., and situated in the borough town of Great Yarmouth, in Nor-folk. The drawings and engravings by H. Shaw, F.S.A. Small folio. London, 1838.

PETIT, V.—Châteaux de la Vallée de la Loire des XVe, XVIe, et com-mencement du XVIIe siècles. Folio. Paris, 1857, *et seq.*

PFNOR ET RAMÉE.—Châteaux de la Renaissance. Monographie du Château de Heidelberg. Folio. Paris, 1857.

BERTY, A.—La Renaissance Monumentale en France. Spécimens de composition et d'ornementation architectoniques empruntés aux édifices construits depuis le règne de Charles VIII, jusqu'à celui de Louis XIV. 4to. Paris, 1858.

The Vatican. Bramante. Raphael. Julio Romano. Oil and Fresco. Venice. The Lombardi. Benvenuto Cellini. Alessandro Vittoria. Majolica-ware. Bernard Palissy. Illustrated Books. Copyright in Designs. General Education of the Decorator.

LECTURE IV.—THE ELIZABETHAN—THE LOUIS QUATORZE.

The Elizabethan, the English version of the Renaissance, a partial elaboration of the Tracery or Strap-work, and the Cartouches or scrolled Shield-work of that style. Examples from Old English Man-sions. Palladio. Inigo Jones. Sir Christopher Wren. Grinling Gibbons.

The Louis Quatorze (1643—1715), of Italian Origin. The Scroll and Shell chief characteristics. General Debasement of Classical Orna-ment; mere play of Light and Shade; Decorations in the Flat super-seded by Stucco, and Colour by Gold. Versailles.

The Louis Quinze (1715—74). Disregard of Symmetry. The Rococo, the Coquillage; all flat surfaces in ornamental details antagonistic to the Louis Quatorze varieties. General Debasement of Ornament. Total want of Individuality of Design. Munich, a new Revival—Ludwig I. Gaertner and Klenze.

RICHARDSON, C. J.—Architectural Remains of the Reigns of Elizabeth and James I., from accurate Drawings and Measurements taken from existing Specimens. Folio. London, 1840.

———— Studies from Old English Mansions, their Furniture, Gold and Silver Plate, &c. 5 vols. small folio. London, 1841—48.

NASH, J.—The Mansions of England in the Olden Time. 4 vols. folio. London, 1839—49.

WARING AND MACQUOID.—Examples of Architectural Art in Italy and Spain, chiefly of the 13th and 16th centuries. Folio. London, 1850.

WARING, J. B.—Art-Treasures of the United Kingdom; consisting of Examples selected from the Manchester Art-Treasures Exhibition, 1857. With descriptive Essays by Owen Jones, M. Digby Wyatt, A. W. Franks, J. C. Robinson, George Scharf, jun., and J. B. Waring. 4to. London, 1857.

———— The Arts connected with Architecture, illustrated by examples in Central Italy, from the 13th to the 15th century. Folio. London, 1858.

WORNUM, R. N.—Catalogue of Ornamental Casts, in the possession of the Department of Science and Art. Third Division: Renaissance Styles. With Illustrations on Wood, engraved by the Female Students of the Wood-Engraving Class. Published by Authority. 8vo. London, 1854.

Marble Panel, Santa Maria de' Miracoli, Venice, by Tullio Lombardi, c. 1500.

THE term Renaissance is used in a double sense: in a general sense implying the revival of art, and specially signifying a peculiar style of ornament, that is, implying both an epoch and a style. The original idea of the

Rinascimento, or re-birth, which is the literal meaning of the term, was purely architectural; the restoration of classical ornament did not immediately follow the restoration of the classical orders, though this was the eventual result. This is an important consideration, for unless we bear constantly in mind that the original revival was simply that of the classical orders of architecture in the place of the middle-age styles, the apparent inconsistencies we shall meet with in the ornamental details of the Renaissance will be liable to confuse us. The Renaissance styles, therefore, are only those styles of ornament which were associated with the gradual revival of the ancient art of Greece and Rome, which was not really accomplished until the sixteenth century, in that finished style the Cinquecento.

The course of ancient and modern art has been much the same; both commenced in the symbolic, and ended in the sensuous. The essence of all middle-age art was symbolism, and the transition from the symbolism to the unalloyed principles of beauty is the great feature of the revival: art was wholly separated from religion in the Renaissance, but this transition was only gradually developed.

It was in Italy that these new styles were almost necessarily developed. Two distinct schools were flourishing there in the twelfth century: the pure Byzantine at Venice, and the Siculo-Norman in the south, containing all the Saracenic elements, not excluding even the inscriptions. From these and the introduction of natural forms wholly irrespective of symbolism arose a new style composed almost exclusively of foliage and tracery.

This change was due to the gradually growing influence of the Saracenic, not as an absolute style, but as affording new elements of beauty, especially its varied and intricate interlacings, which were so very prominent for a while as to constitute the chief characteristic of a new style, the first step of the transition from middle-age to modern art; known from its mean time, about the year 1300, as the *Trecento*.

The new life and activity displayed by Italy at this period was in some degree owing to the Crusades, and more especially to the Latin conquest of Constantinople in the year 1204, which displayed many treasures of ancient art to the Venetians, whose taste was already sufficiently cultivated to appreciate their value; and four ancient bronze horses, a Christian trophy of this Venetian crusade, still adorn the façade of St. Mark's.

Venice, already rich in Byzantine works, appears to have taken the lead also in the dawning revival of classical art; and the Venetians seem likewise to have contributed more than any others to its most finished development, the Cinquecento. The Venetians and the Italians generally, controlled by no trammels of tradition, added their own beginnings of natural imitations, to Christian or to Pagan elements indiscriminately; the prestige of a thousand years was broken; the classical forms prevailed, and the *Quattrocento*, the first great style of the Renaissance, was established. From this time, the fifteenth century, we have done with all Christian forms and elements in Italy, in the ordinary details of ornamental art.

The first of these modern innovations is the transition style, the Trecento; which may be considered a negative style, as its peculiarity consists in its exclusion of certain hitherto common ornamental elements.

Gate of Baptistery, Florence.

The great features of this style are its intricate tracery or interlacings, and delicate scroll-work of conventional foliage, the style being but a slight remove from a combination of the Byzantine and Saracenic, the symbolism of both being equally excluded; the foliage and floriage, however, are not exclusively conventional, and it comprises a fair rendering of the classical orders, with *the restoration of the round arch.* Nicola Pisano, Andrea Taffi, Giotto, and their contemporaries, were the great masters of this style, and the Church of San Francesco at Assisi and the Cathedral of Florence are fine examples of it.

In the Quattrocento, the next style, we have a far more positive revival. Lorenzo Ghiberti may, perhaps, be instanced as its great exponent or representative in ornamental art. Filippo Calendario and Antonio Riccio, called Briosco, contemporary with Ghiberti, are likewise important names of this period : they were engaged on the new Ducal Palace at Venice, which is most comprehensive in the character of its ornamental details.

The bronze gates of the Baptistery of San Giovanni, by Ghiberti (1425-52), exhibit one feature of this style in perfection—the prominence of simple natural imitations, which now nearly entirely supersede the conventional representations of previous times. Nature no longer supplied mere suggestions, but afforded directly exact models of imitation, whether fruit, flowers, birds, or animals, all disposed simply with a view to the picturesque or ornamental. The *selection* of the details might still have some typical signification, but this had no influence in the *manner* of their execution, which was as purely imitative as their arrangement was ornamental.

In this style, also, we have the first appearance of cartouches or scrolled shield-work, which became so very prominent in the sixteenth and seventeenth centuries. One of the oldest examples I can refer to is the shield containing the lion of St. Mark, on the water-gate of the Ducal Palace at Venice, perhaps the work of Briosco, in the middle of the fifteenth century; it suggests the idea of the imitation of a sealed parchment, or a MS. illumination.

This kind of decoration certainly seems in some way connected with heraldry—many of its forms are palpably mere armorial shields, which became very common in architectural decoration of a later period, and the fact of such forms being afterwards used as mere elements of ornament does not in any way invalidate such an origin.

There are none of these forms on the gates of Ghiberti; but it abounds with medallions containing portraits, which perform a similar service in the design as the shields in other examples.

Another feature of this Quattrocento style—or what is more especially the Italian Renaissance, as distinct from the Cinquecento—is the introduction, for the first time, of the grotesque arabesque, after the ancient models of Rome and Pompeii: in fact, the style of decoration is now of a very complicated character, though not confused, for we still have the *Trecento* interlacings very largely used as borders, and the scroll, from the petty serpentine character of the previous style, appears with all the fulness of the Roman arabesque, but not yet very prominently introduced.

Although in the Quattrocento the religious symbolism was excluded generally (not absolutely) from the ornamental details, the religious sentiment was by no means absent from the Quattrocento art itself; on the contrary, the Quattrocento is essentially a religious style, but the religious sentiment was transferred from a secondary to a primary object in the design: we have the actual representation instead of the mere symbol. As, for instance, in the second pair of Ghiberti gates—the history of Moses is the principal subject of illustration of these gates—the ornaments are but the decorations to the several panels; so it is in all other great schemes, of which the Certosa of Pavia offers many examples. There is little decoration but what is merely auxiliary to some religious design. It was not so in the Cinquecento; the figures and subjects themselves are a mere part—and often a secondary one—of the ornamental scheme, and the religious element comparatively disappears. We speak of the Renaissance as an Epoch and as a Style, but the only true or literal revival is the Cinquecento; the other varieties contain too many original and extraneous elements to be considered an historical revival.

Bronze. From Door of St. Maclou, Rouen, c. 1542.

THE capricious style, the so-called Renaissance of the
sixteenth century, which was in such good repute with the
jewellers, was far more conspicuous for its cartouches (its
scrolled shield-work) and tracery than for the more natural
or the more classical elements of the style; the beauties
of nature and the standard ornaments of antiquity could
not vie, in the general taste, with either the attraction of
novelty or the charm of indiscriminate variety, especially
with the example of such names as Primaticcio, Holbein,
and Benvenuto Cellini, as its advocates; but in as far as
art and manipulation again attained the ascendency over
symbolism it also was a revival, by reasserting the æsthetic
principle.

Carved Door Panels, from the Château d'Anet; now at the École des Beaux Arts, Paris;
c. 1548.

This third modern style or variety, to which the name of Renaissance by habit more particularly belongs, is essentially a style of varieties, especially in jewellery and in works in relief: it was very general also out of Italy, and especially in France, where it was introduced about the time of Francis I.; and it is still so great a favourite with the French, that French and Renaissance are nearly identical terms. This style is, however, made up chiefly of elements foreign to classical taste, and the essence of the Cinquecento is its rejection of these elements; but before proceeding to the consideration of the latter we will consider what is specially signified by the Renaissance as a style.

Carved Door Panel from the Château d'Anet, now at the Ecole des Beaux Arts, Paris.

It is the style of Benvenuto Cellini. It is also remarkably developed in the remains of the Château d'Anet, near Dreux, in France (about 1548), and other buildings of that time, and it is indeed sometimes designated the Henry II. style.

The mixture of various elements is one of the essentials of this style; these elements are, the classical ornaments; conventional and natural flowers and foliage—the former often of a pure Saracenic character; man and animals, natural and grotesque; cartouches, or pierced and scrolled shields, as above, in great prominence; tracery, independent and developed from the scrolls of the cartouches; and jewel forms. The whole history of art does not afford a parallel mixture of elements. It was popular in the Low Countries at the same time: the Bourse at Antwerp (1531) is one of its earliest examples.

Our own Elizabethan is a partial elaboration of the same style, probably introduced into this country from the Low Countries, the only difference being that the Elizabethan, like that of Henry II. of France, exhibits a very striking preponderance of strap-and-shield-work; but this was a gradual result, and what we now term the Elizabethan was not thoroughly developed until the time of James I., when the pierced shields even outbalanced the strap-work. The pure Elizabethan is much nearer allied to the continental styles of the time—classical ornaments, but rude in detail, occasional scroll and arabesque work, and the tracery or strap-work, holding a much more prominent place than the pierced and scrolled shields. For the want of better information these two features are sufficient to date a building—the tracery or strap-work, without the shield-work, will indicate the time of Elizabeth; the predominance of shield-work that of James I., as at Wallaton and Yarmouth, Elizabethan; Crewe Hall and Canonbury House, Islington, of the time of James. In Crewe Hall, an early work, and attributed to Inigo Jones, the shield-work is not very prominent.

Such are four varieties of the revival, distinct from its perfect form, the Cinquecento. A design containing all the elements of this period is properly called Renaissance. If a design contain only the tracery and foliage of the

151   From the old Guard Chamber, Westminster. c. 1600.

Ceiling, Loseley House Surrey.

Carved Stone, Doorway, Crewe Hall, Cheshire.

period it would be more properly called Trecento; if it contain, besides these, elaborate natural imitations, festoons, scroll-work, and occasional symmetrical arabesques, it is of the Quattrocento, the Italian Renaissance of the fifteenth century; and if it display a decided prominence

In the "Ancient Parlour," Holland House.

of strap-work and shield-work it is Elizabethan. In all these styles the evidence of their Byzantine and Saracenic origin is constantly preserved—in the tracery, in the scroll-work and foliage, in the rendering of classical ornaments; and in the earlier varieties, in the shape of the panels containing religious illustrations, which even to the close of the Quattrocento are of pure Byzantine shapes, as they abound in the manuscripts.

The Renaissance is, therefore, something more approximate to a combination of previous styles than a revival of any in particular. It is the first example of selection that we find, and it is a style that was developed solely on æsthetic principles, from a love of the forms and harmonies themselves, as varieties of effect or arrangements of beauty, not because they had any particular signification, or from any superstitious attachment to them as ancestral heirlooms. The decorators of the Renaissance were, in fact, the first *artists* in ornamental art since the classic periods ; they suffered no limits or restrictions but those of harmony or beauty, according to their own perception of the beautiful.

ELIZABETHAN. North Entrance, Wollaton.

CHAPTER XV.

THE CINQUECENTO.

∵

ILLUSTRATED LITERATURE.

PISTOLESI, E.—The Vatican described and illustrated.

Il Vaticano descritto ed illustrato. 8 vols. folio. Rome, 1829—38.

RAPHAEL.—The Arabesques of the Vatican. Oblong folio, 32 plates, *n. d.*

———— Loggie di Rafaele nel Vaticano. Drawn by Camporesi, and engraved by Volpato and others. 61 plates. Altas folio. Roma, 1772—76.

SUYS ET HAUDEBOURT.—Palais Massimi à Rome. Plans, coupes, élévations, profils, voûtes, plafonds, &c. des deux Palais Massimi, dessinés et publiés par F. T. Suys et L. P. Haudebourt. Folio. Paris, *n. d.*

BETTONI, N.—Tombs and Monuments of Italy.

Le Tombe ed i Monumenti illustri d'Italia. 2 vols. 4to. Milan, 1822—23.

MAGAZZARI, G.—The most select Ornaments of Bologna.

Raccolta de' più scelti Ornati sparsi per la città di Bologna. Ob. 4to. Bologna, 1827.

ANTONELLI, G.—A Collection of the best Venetian Ornaments.

Collezione de' Migliori Ornamenti antichi, sparsi nella città di Venezia. Ob. 4to. Venice, 1831.

DIEDO E ZANOTTO.—Sepulchral Monuments of Venice.

Novanta Monumenti cospicui di Venezia illustrati dal Cav. Antonio Diedo e da Francesco Zanotto. Folio. Milan, 1839.

CICOGNARA, L.—The most remarkable Buildings and Monuments of Venice.

Le Fabbriche e i Monumenti cospicui di Venezia; illustrati da Leopoldo Cicognara, da Antonio Diedo, e da Giannantonio Selva. Con notabili aggiunte e note. 2nd edition, 2 vols. large folio. Venice, 1840.

LETAROUILLY, P.—Edifices of Modern Rome, with Details.

Edifices de Rome Moderne, ou Recueil des Palais, Maisons, Eglises,

Couvents, et autres Monuments publics et particuliers les plus remarquables de la Ville de Rome. 3 vols. folio ; text, 2 vols. 4to. Paris, 1840, *et seq.*

Tosi AND Becchio.—Altars, Tabernacles, and Sepulchral Monuments of the Fifteenth and Sixteenth Centuries, existing at Rome. Folio. Lagny, 1843.

Bergamo, Stefano da.—Wood Carvings from the Choir of the Monastery of San Pietro at Perugia, 1535 ; said to be from designs by Raphael.

Gli Ornati del Coro della Chiesa di S. Pietro dei Monaci Cassinesi di Perugia, intagliati in Legno da Stefano da Bergamo sopra i disegni di Raffaello Santi da Urbino, ora per la' prima volta tutti raccolti incisi a contorno e pubblicati. Folio. Rome, 1845.

Gruner, L.—Specimens of Ornamental Art, selected from the best Models of the Classical Epochs. Illustrated with 80 plates, with descriptive text, by Emil Braun. By Authority. Folio. London, 1850.

———— Fresco Decorations and Stuccoes of Churches and Palaces in Italy, during the Fifteenth and Sixteenth Centuries, with Descriptions by Lewis Gruner, K.A. New edition, largely augmented by numerous plates, plain and coloured. Folio. London, 1854.

———— Lo Scaffale : or Presses in the Sacristy of the Church of Sta. Maria delle Grazie at Milan. Illustrations of the painted decoration by Bernardino Luini. Folio. London, 1859.

Louvre.—Le Napoléonium. Monographie du Louvre et des Tuileries réunis, avec une notice historique et archéologique. Fol. Paris, 1856.

Contant et Filippi.—Parallèle des principaux Théâtres modernes de l'Europe. Folio. Paris, 1859, *et seq.*

Calliat, V.—Parallèle des Maisons de Paris. Nouvelle période de 1850 à 1860. Folio. Paris, 1860.

We may now proceed to the consideration of the Cinquecento, which as an art development is the most perfect of all the modern styles. The term Cinquecento does not imply simply sixteenth-century art, but the most prominent style of the sixteenth century ; and it is the real goal of the Renaissance, to which all the efforts of the fifteenth century tended. The varieties we have just been examining are but its wanderings by the way, for want of sufficiently conspicuous landmarks. It was only after a great accumulation of materials that it was

From the Martinengo Tomb, Brescia. c. 1530.

164 From the Façade of Santa Maria de' Miracoli, Brescia. c. 1530.

possible to appreciate thoroughly the spirit of the ancient arabesques.

These came at last out of the excavations of ancient monuments at Rome and elsewhere at the close of the fifteenth century—the new revival was developed chiefly by the sculptors of the North, and the painters of Central Italy. The true spirit of ancient art was only now thoroughly comprehended, and all extraneous elements were successively excluded ; but with such capacities as those of Raphael, Julio Romano, the Lombardi, Bramante, or Michelangelo, applied to extricate it from its long entombment, no wonder that it started suddenly into new life, and grew even into a more splendid development than it had ever known, perhaps, in its most gorgeous Roman period.

However, it would be unjust towards the great quattro-cento masters to give all the credit of this accomplished style of art to even such names as Raphael, Julio Romano, or Bramante.

The efforts of these masters were at first little or no improvements upon the works of their immediate predecessors, the great *quattrocentisti*, such as Baccio Pintelli, Pietro Perugino, Francia, Bernardino Luini, and Pinturicchio—the two last scarcely inferior to Julio Romano himself, the prince of decorators ; and the Lombardi, Agostino Busti, Andrea Sansovino, and other sculptors of the north of Italy, may claim, perhaps, equal rank in their art.

The principal monuments of the Cinquecento in painting are the Vatican Loggie, the Villa Madama at Rome, and the ducal palaces at Mantua : the churches of Venice,

Verona, and Brescia, afford the best examples of Sculpture.
The Loggie of Raphael are the arcade of the second story
of the Court of San Damaso ; they were executed about
1515, by Julio Romano, Gian Francesco Penni, and
Giovanni da Udine ; the last painted the birds and animals,
the abundance of which is a very striking feature in the
Vatican arabesques.

These *arabesques* of Raphael, or, as they were originally
called, *grotesques*, from being chiefly discovered in the
ancient grottoes, are said to have been directly suggested
by some ancient remains in the Baths of Titus. They
appear to have given a great impetus to this style of
decoration, for they are the first of their kind on an
extensive scale ; and, even in their character, they differ
very widely from the quattrocento arabesques, which were
derived chiefly from ancient sculpture and from the MSS.,
and are very much more formal in their arrangements
and detail.

However, though the arabesques themselves are of the
cinquecento character, in the exuberance and beauty of
the curves and foliations, the entire decorations of the
pilasters are far from being of pure style.

In establishing a style from examples, made with only
a general regard to its most prominent characteristics,
there is, of course, much to reject before we have a
characteristic illustration of the style ; and the Christian
symbols, and other arbitrary forms, which we occasionally
find in Raphael's arabesques, must be scrupulously excluded, or the Cinquecento becomes merged into the
mixed Renaissance, which led to it, and the distinction
of style is lost.

J. F. Swallow, del.

From Carved Oak Panels in the Louvre, Paris.   c. 1520.

176

From a Marble Fountain in the Louvre, Paris.   Italian.   1508.

The Vatican pilasters, like the designs of Luini and Pinturicchio, are of a transition character. The Villa Madama at Rome, and the Ducal Palaces at Mantua, display designs of equal variety of effect, with a greater unity of character in the details. They are the work of Giovanni da Udine and Julio Romano, the same artists who executed those of the Vatican Loggie, but in these later works many of the licences in the Vatican arabesques have been in a great measure avoided. They are of a more unmixed classical character; the scrolls are particularly fine.

Some of the Vatican compositions, from their mechanical absurdities, are ludicrous and offensive, while the more extravagant designs in the later works are the most fanciful; and, indeed, the grotesque is perhaps the most prominent feature of the cinquecento arabesque.

The designer, like the poet, has his licence with regard to possibilities or probabilities. A mere natural improbability, where natural imitation is in no degree essential, is the privilege of the fancy; but mechanical disproportions and impossibilities, violations of the most palpable laws of gravity, cannot be otherwise than offensive. Nothing can bring them within the range of good taste, as they are essentially obnoxious to æsthetic sensibility, which is the truest test of propriety in art, the effect being analogous to a discord in music. We may be extremely grotesque or fanciful without being ridiculous.

There need be no limit to our chimeras, for nature is not their test; but if we combine monsters in our scrolls, or place animals upon the tendrils of plants, we should at least proportion them in size to the strength of the

R

tendril upon which they are placed. This is not observed in many of the Vatican arabesques, and it is occasionally disregarded, also, in the later works of Mantua; yet these are, in other respects, the standard types of the cinquecento arabesques, as developed in painting.

It was this same fault of painful disproportion which Pliny and Vitruvius found with the arabesques of Pompeii, which display anomalies not so much as approached by even the worst specimens of modern times. Natural foliage teaches us that the greater the burden the thicker the stem; the gradual diminishing of the stem as its burden decreases, is one of the essential beauties of foliage. And this law is admirably observed in nearly all the best examples of the Cinquecento, especially in the sculpture; but there are otherwise good specimens in which it is not observed. It is necessarily a condition peculiar to arabesque scroll-work; for in a continuous scroll we do not require this variation of thickness, as it is a mere ornamental repetition, every portion in itself being complete; and as it is indeterminate, no portion of the curve has more to do than another. This is an essential difference; in the arabesque curves the scroll or spiral is always completed; it is a determinate figure, and its elegance or lightness will depend upon the relative proportions of the stem.

This arabesque scroll-work is the most prominent feature of the Cinquecento; and with this it combines in its elements every other feature of classical art, with the unlimited choice of natural and conventional imitations from the entire animal and vegetable kingdoms, both arbitrarily disposed and combined.

171   From the Monument to Louis XII., St. Denis near Paris. c. 1520.

Another of its features is its beautiful variations of ancient standard ornaments, as the anthemion especially, of which there are some admirable Cinquecento examples.

The guilloche or plat, the fret, and the acanthus scroll are likewise favourites, and occur in many varieties. The Cinquecento appears, indeed, to be the special province of the curve in its infinite play of arabesque; but in all its developments it is in the form of some natural object or artificial combination. The cartouches and strapwork wholly disappear from the best examples. In all the extensive works in sculpture of the north of Italy, from about 1480 until 1550, such forms are extremely rare; and in defining the Cinquecento as a style, their exclusion becomes an essential condition. Absolute works of art, such as vases, and implements and instruments of all kinds, are prominent elements of the cinquecento arabesque; but cartouches and strapwork as unauthorised by ancient practice, are necessarily excluded from the style as a presumed ancient revival.

Carved Wood. Château de Gaillon, France. c. 1505.

It is, however, in sculpture, perhaps, that we must look for the purest examples of this style, as regards the mere elaboration of form; and among the cinquecento sculptors none paid more attention to ornament than the Lombardi of Venice and Agostino Busti of Milan. Venice abounds with the works of the Lombardi, of whom Tullio is prominently distinguished. His monumental bas-reliefs have, perhaps, never been surpassed for their exquisite spirit and delicacy of execution: and even in their details they are unsurpassed by the best examples of antiquity. Sometimes they consist of fine elaborations of the pure classic acanthus scroll; at others, and more commonly, of the standard arabesques, with the interspersing of grotesque figures and animals, and occasionally of simple curves, with ordinary natural foliations, combining a strict imitation with a masterly freedom of execution.

Another chief feature of the Cinquecento is the admirable play of colour in its arabesques and scrolls; and it is worthy of note, that the three secondary colours, orange, green, and purple, perform the chief parts in all the coloured decorations. Its great leading form, the acanthus scroll or foliated spiral, is sometimes a complete iris, with its beautiful variety of tints, as in some of Julio Romano's decorations at Mantua. And where we have but two colours, we have constantly complements.

Indeed, the Cinquecento may be considered the culminating style in ornamental art, as presenting the most perfect forms and the most pleasing varieties, nature and art vying with each other in their efforts to attract and gratify the eye. It appeals only to the sense of beauty. All its efforts are directly made to attain the most attractive effects, without any intent to lead the mind to an ulterior end, as is the case with the Byzantine and other symbolic styles. The cinquecento forms are supposed to be symbols of beauty alone; and it is a remarkable concession to the ancients, that the moderns, to attain this result, were compelled to recur to their works; and it is only now in the contemplation of this consummate style, that the term Renaissance becomes quite intelligible. The Renaissance, or rebirth of ornament, is accomplished in the Cinquecento; still the term is not altogether ill appropriated to the earlier styles, because these were really the stepping-stones to the Cinquecento; and, as already explained, in them, also, the æsthetic was substituted for the symbolic. The principles, therefore, were identical, though from imperfect apprehension, elements strange to the classical period were generally admitted; it was a revival of principle though not of element.

The Cinquecento very generally pervaded manufactures for a time in France as well as Italy, though for a much shorter period than its great beauties and applicability would seem to justify. The arms and armour, and the pottery or majolica wares of the time afford some of the finest examples of the style.

It was, however, not long successfully pursued: it appears to be too exact in its details, and too comprehensive in its range of elements, for the ordinary grasp of the decorator, whether from the kingdoms of nature or the realms of art, poetry, and history; every form being excluded having neither wit nor beauty to recommend it. It required too much from the designer's powers, for, besides a familiarity with the art of classic antiquity, it exacted a considerable acquaintance with the figure, as well as a mastery over the animal and vegetable forms generally.

Accordingly, already in the sixteenth century, ornamental art fell back to what it was before that time; and from the middle of the sixteenth century, as illustrated by the works of Alessandro Vittoria, Nicola dei Conti, Alfonso Alberghetti, and Benvenuto Cellini, we again find the promiscuous mixture of forms of all kinds with a prominence of the cartouche, as in the ordinary Renaissance, which, from its far less definite character, gave greater liberty to the artist, in accordance with his own vague notions of variety, the attainment of which seems now, and for a long period, to have usurped every other purpose.

The Cinquecento is essentially an Italian style, though in some few instances good examples are found out of Italy, especially in France; as the monument to Louis XII. in the church of St. Denis, near Paris, and several examples at Rouen, and at the Château de Gaillon, Normandy. These were, however, either carried out by Italians, or directly from some Italian example.

The ordinary ornament of the Renaissance was at the same time very common in the North and West, and was evidently much spread by the little works with ornamental marginal woodcuts published frequently in the sixteenth century, and expressly for designers for manufactures; as in the case of the edition of Alciati's

Emblems, published at Lyons in 1551, of which there is a copy in the Library of the Department.

Chimney-piece, Louvre. By Germain Pilon.

CHAPTER XVI.

FOR a century after the development of the Cinquecento, there was little individuality in the practice of ornamental art. Architecture itself was completely domineered by a mere classical pedantry, rule and measure usurped the place of expression. Towards the close of the seventeenth century, however, a new style commenced to develop itself (the Louis Quatorze), essentially an ornamental style, and differing very materially in principle from nearly all that preceded it, its chief aim being effect by a brilliant play of light and shade ; colour or mere beauty of form in detail having no part in it whatever. This style, like most others of modern times, arose in Italy ; and we may, perhaps, look upon the Chiesa del Gesù, or Jesus Church, at Rome, as its type or model. The principal decorators of this church were Giacomo della Porta, Pietro da Cortona, and Father Pozzi, author of the well-known Jesuits' perspective.

Of the vague character of the intermediate style, after the decline of the Cinquecento, the various nautilus-shells are good examples, something of the Renaissance, Elizabethan, and Louis Quatorze combined.

The great medium of the Louis Quatorze (1643-1715)

was gilt stucco-work, which, for a while, seems to have almost wholly superseded decorative painting; and this absence of colour in the principal decorations of the period seems to have led to its more striking characteristic, —infinite play of light and shade.

Such being the aim of the style, exact symmetry in the parts was no longer essential, and, accordingly, in the Louis Quatorze varieties, we, for the first time, occasionally find symmetry systematically avoided. This feature was gradually more and more elaborated, till it became essential in the Louis Quinze, and ultimately led to that debased yet popular style, the Rococo, in which symmetry, either in the balance of the whole or in the details of the parts, seems to have been quite out of place.

Versailles is the great repertory of the Louis Quatorze; but the whole was evidently intended to present a gorgeous classical scheme of decoration. Foreign elements, however, and foreign treatment, both found their place; and it is to these foreign features that the decorations owe their individuality. They are the constant and peculiar combination of the scroll and shell—the anthemion treated as a shell, and a small scroll, sometimes plain and sometimes clothed in acanthus foliations. All the other elements of the style are classical, such as we find them treated in the Cinquecento, with some slightly modified new varieties. The fiddle-shape combination of scrolls is, perhaps, a legacy of the ordinary Renaissance.

The Louis Quinze (1715-74) does not much differ from the Louis Quatorze in its elements; but yet, from a certain manner of treatment, must be considered as

S

distinct in a discrimination of styles. It differs in this, that the merely characteristic elements of the Louis Quatorze became paramount in the Louis Quinze; all its details, instead of coming direct from the Cinquecento, or Renaissance, came immediately from the French schemes of the preceding reign; the diverging, therefore, from the original types became ever wider.

In comparing good examples of these two styles, we shall find that the broad acanthus foliations or featherings of the scroll in the Louis Quatorze have become very much elongated, approaching the flag or fleur-de-lis leaf and the palm-branch in the Louis Quinze.

Perhaps the great feature of the later style, and that to which it owes its bizarre character, as much as any other, is its rejection of symmetry in its details, even in the most central and prominent places; a feature which until now would have been considered a capital defect in a design: such is the caprice of fashion. But as a *general* play of light and shade was the chief aim of the style, it was little injured by a want of symmetry in details, always too indefinite for special attention.

The play of light and shade in sudden and varied contrasts is so essential an element of the Louis Quatorze styles, that they do not admit flat surfaces in any of their ornamental details; all are concave or convex, perfectly smooth but never flat—even the anthemion in these styles becomes a hollow shell. They thus contrast very strongly with the Elizabethan, in which flat surfaces in the details abound, as in its infinite strap-work; even in the cartouches, or pierced and scrolled shields, the curved planes are flat. All such members in the Louis

Quatorze styles would be channelled or moulded. This
constant varying of the surface gives every point of view
its high lights and brilliant contrasts; and for this reason
stucco superseded decorations in the flat, and gold colour,
in all Louis Quatorze designs.

Still the Louis Quatorze is not altogether unfit for
decorations in the flat, but it is limited to designs on
a small scale, and colour is in these cases indispensable;
this is exemplified in the metal marquetry of Boule, the
forms depending on their contrast with their ground;
and by the designs of Watteau.

Watteau, in fact, reduced the Louis Quatorze to colour,
and brought it more generally within the province of
manufactures. He used the elements of the style for
the frames or boundaries of small panels,—pastoral or rural
scenes, which he surrounded by fantastical borders, of scrolls,
fruit, flowers, and foliage, birds, insects, and animals.

The spirit of these Louis Quatorze styles, and, perhaps,
more particularly the Louis Quinze, pervaded all manufactures, more or less, until the Revolution, not only
in France but in many parts of Europe. Meissonier,
Claude Ballin, and Le Pautre were, each in his way,
the most popular designers of their time. Even in Italy,
Bernini used the designs of Le Pautre for external and
internal decoration: he was the greatest master of the
Louis Quatorze in its adaptation to ornamental sculpture,
independent of architecture; his bravura of line was
remarkable, and all tending, by the constant alternation
of the round and hollow, or projecting and receding
shapes, to the one great aim of the style—a lively play
of light and shade.

The chief distinction between these two styles is the want of symmetry in the Louis Quinze: it is in many of its examples a mere and almost random dispersion of the scroll and shell, mixed only with that peculiar crimping or shell-work, the coquillage. Still with these elements beautiful effects were produced, when only a slight attention was bestowed upon the arrangement of the masses; but when this last was neglected, the designs became a mere mass of vagaries, of indescribable forms, and the Rococo was displayed in the perfection of the bizarre in ornament, and in which the thread of the historic styles is at last completely run out.

CONCLUSION.

In this review of the ornamental devices of thirty-five centuries, we have certainly had every variety of expression that the human mind is familiar with. I have dwelt, of course, upon the leading styles only; any other course would have been impossible with an ordinary degree of clearness. By converting mere varieties into styles, we should so multiply the number of ornamental expressions that the student would probably be so much confused as to be unable to eliminate even the generic varieties of ornamental art. Thus, I do not pretend, in this review of the styles, to have explained more than the great leading developments of ancient, middle-age, and modern art.

In the early period, with the Egyptians, we found symbolism, richness of material, with simplicity of arrangement, and an artistic crudity, as the prominent characteristics. In the second, or Greek period, we have exclusively an æsthetic aim, with general beauty of effect, and uniform excellence of detail throughout; everywhere displaying the highest artistic skill. In the third, or Roman period, still with an æsthetic aim, we have equal skill, with a taste for a more gorgeous detail and more general magnificence.

In the Byzantine,—the first style of the second period, —we go back to at first an almost exclusive symbolism, which, however, in the course of a century or two, is elaborated into a style of a very gorgeous general effect,— combining the æsthetic with the symbolic—partly owing to richness of materials; but as prejudice was gradually overcome, a comprehensive and beautiful style was ultimately developed in the sixth century, but nearly always displaying, perhaps, more skill in its general effects than in its details.

The Saracenic is the same in principle,—a gorgeous general effect, without any remarkable merit of detail: it is made up of an infinite number of minute contrasts of light and shade and colour,—something like a formal flower-garden, wanting the simplicity and grandeur of natural scenery; but it is capable of very beautiful general effects on a small scale.

In the Gothic, again,—the last of the middle-age styles, —symbolism more than divides the field with art, and induces much of that crudity of detail which must be the inevitable result of a divided attention. The general effects are often grand; but the details are ill expressed, and inferior.

In the Renaissance,—the herald of the modern styles, and, like the classical styles, purely æsthetic,—we have, at first, the natural vagaries of an unaccustomed freedom; which, however, eventually settled into a genuine revival of the most finished style of antiquity,—the Cinquecento. Then came the final decline,—mere love of display, gold and glitter: such is the Louis Quatorze,—still, prodigiously clever in the means it took to accomplish its effects.

The Louis Quatorze is more general in its aim than any style whatever : thus its details, provided they generated sufficient contrasts of light and shade, were of no individual consequence. Accordingly we find, after a little time, that all detail is absolutely neglected, and with it all study : and in the absurd Rococo,—the very natural result of this general neglect,—we have designs made up of details so without meaning and individuality, as to defy description. They are Rococo ; we can come no nearer to them ; and with this Rococo, the first term of existence, the last of the nine lives of ornamental art expires.

This vast store of materials, taken in the mass, without selection or order, is a mere chaos ; and so far from creating variety, will, unless classified into schools or styles, engender only a mere uniform repetition of confusion.

This is the view, then, with which we study the history of art,—to discriminate and individualise the styles of the various epochs; and by thus developing distinct characters, multiply to an equal extent our means of viewing nature, and our powers, consequently, of representation. The real result of historical knowledge, therefore, is not the mere copying of what has been done before, but the acquisition of a power which not only supersedes all copying, but which alone will insure the production of that variety of ornamental design which, the simplest theory must make manifest, is the ostensible effort of every designer.

Had the knowledge of styles been a little more disseminated in the present day, we should not have found the Louis XV., and the Rococo, as the prevailing English tastes of the Great Exhibition of 1851. In fault of his-

torical knowledge, and its consequently enlarged views
of art, the designer has been reduced to merely copying
his neighbour : hence the still paramount importance in
this country of the last great historic style of France,—
the Louis XV.,—in silver, in wood-carving, in carpets,
damasks,—even in lace, also, and in many other branches.

The great lesson we may learn from a study of the
characteristics of styles is, that our designs want individuality : they are too general, too much alike : we require
something more than mere sprigs and colonnades, or conventional scrolls. We want both systems of detail and
systems of arrangement. A picture is not an ornament ;
but every flower, however simple,—and, indeed, every leaf,
—is capable of being converted into an ornament by the
mere aid of repetition on a geometrical basis ; and the same
forms may be beautifully varied by altering this basis ; and
again, by new judicious combinations of colour, applied to
the same geometric scheme.

We should work on the principles of construction of
natural objects, independent of their individualities of
development. The value of such a system in ornamental
design is incalculable : but it is only by a knowledge of
the characteristics of styles,—the standard types of all
ages, that even system will effect that variety and individuality of expression, which alone will secure a perma-
nent gratification or success.

The great success of the Greeks was not more than
commensurate with the strict adherence to principles of
beauty upon which even their slightest efforts depended.
The cheap manufactures of antiquity, as the ordinary
Greek terra-cottas, were cheap by reason of the nature of

their material, not from any neglect of care in their manufacture.

The ancient prosperity of the Samians is a remarkable instance of the great national benefit to be derived from the judicious application of art to manufactures, and is worthy the emulation of their modern British competitors. The small island of Samos, by its potteries alone, carried on an important trade with all the great cities of the Greek and Roman empires, and thus was enabled to compete in splendour and luxury with the greatest states of the ancient world. Herodotus (iv. 152) speaks of the unparalleled fortune of a Samian merchant. It was the first Greek state that attained celebrity in the arts. Its temple of Juno, the famous *Heræum*, was perhaps the most celebrated art-repository of antiquity, and was itself a work of extraordinary grandeur. The same Greek historian (iii. 60) speaks of it as the largest temple he ever saw, though it was constructed entirely of marble. The workers in metal and the painters were equal in renown to the sculptors and architects of Samos. All this magnificence was but the fruit of its industrial ingenuity, its skilful ship-building, its enterprising commerce, its matchless potteries. The skill of its potters made the very soil they trod upon more precious than gold. This earthenware of Samos carried its commerce over every sea, to every port, until its merchants became princes, and this small island-state was conspicuous among the richest nations of the world. It was this distinction, this political pre-eminence, which excited the jealousy of its more powerful neighbours : and with its freedom, its commerce and its prosperity declined together.

T

The sun still shines on the fruitful valleys of Samos, and it still abounds in the valuable clay of which its ancient potteries were manufactured; but its population has declined into a mere scattered and rude peasantry : its potters have departed; the genial clay without the skilful hand to fashion it is of little avail.

Such was Samos when it directed its energies to the arts ; such is it now that all cultivation of art has ceased. It was but the judicious application of art to industry that made this small Levantine island once the illustrious rival of great empires.

THE END.

PRINTED BY VIRTUE AND CO., LIMITED, CITY ROAD, LONDON.

www.ingramcontent.com/pod-product-compliance
Lightning Source LLC
Chambersburg PA
CBHW030552040726
47497CB00008B/2682